Entrepreneur William Goodspeed of East Haddam, 1815 – 1882, controlled finances, shipping, and shipbuilding. In 1876, he initiated the building of the playhouse, employing architect Jabez Comstock. The top two stories of this six-story, Second Empire structure contained the theater. The remainder contained a general store, post office, and shipping offices. The rugged wharf accommodated the steamboats that brought actors, audience and freight.

The Opera House opened 24 October 1877 with productions of *Charles I, Box and Cox, and Turn Him Out!*. Opera was never billed at the Opera House, but the theater hosted Vaudeville, lectures, and dances. Josh Billings and Henry Ward Beecher spoke here, and Harriet Beecher Stowe's adaptation of Uncle Tom's Cabin was performed.

Following Goodspeed's death the Opera House underwent a reversal of fortunes. The theater closed in 1920. The building served as general store, militia base during World War I, and, finally, as storage depot for the Connecticut Department of Transportation, which gutted the ground floor for parking vehicles. When Connecticut condemned the building, citizens, led by Mrs. Alfred Howe Terry and Mrs. Paul Libby Kaye, undertook to restore the Opera House to its former glory. Frederick Palmer served as architect.

The *Goodspeed Opera House Foundation* and *Goodspeed Musicals* non-profit organization, founded in 1959, bought the building from the state for one dollar. After four years of fundraising and restoration, the rededication took place on 18 June 1963. The first performance was the musical, *Oh, Lady, Lady!*, attended by Governor John Dempsey.

Under longtime director, Michael Price, the Goodspeed and its satellite, the Norma Terris Theater, produce up to six musicals per season. Sixteen new plays have continued to Broadway, including *Annie, Man of La Mancha*, and *Shenandoah*. More than a dozen Tony's have been awarded to Goodspeed productions, and *Goodspeed Musicals* has received two special Tony's for outstanding achievement. The National Register of Historic Places listed the Goodspeed in 1971. Visit them at www.goodspeed.org. For tickets, call 860 – 873 – 8668.

LANDMARKS
YOU *MUST* VISIT
In Southeast Connecticut

Constant Waterman

Written & Illustrated
By
Constant Waterman

LANDMARKS YOU MUST VISIT IN SOUTHEAST CONNECTICUT

Text and illustrations Copyright 2010 by Matthew Goldman aka Constant Waterman

ISBN 978-0-615-37342-3

My illustrations of the Chester-Hadlyme Ferry, Breakwater Lighthouse, Ledge Lighthouse, New London Harbor Lighthouse, Morgan Point Lighthouse, and Stonington Harbor Lighthouse first appeared in THE JOURNALS OF CONSTANT WATERMAN: PADDLING, POLING, AND SAILING FOR THE LOVE OF IT by Matthew Goldman, copyright 2007. They have been published here courtesy of Breakaway Books. www.breakawaybooks.com

Author photo by John Wray

Cover design and layout by Sandy and Marilena Vaccaro www.smart-graphics.com

Printed by: bookprinting revolution www.bookprintingrevolution.com

First edition

Dedication

To Carol Kimball

Grande Dame of local history

ACKNOWLEDGEMENTS

I am indebted to the following for their help:

The Historical Societies of Stonington, Mystic River, Deep River,
Noank, East Haddam, Chester; the Rathbun Library in East Haddam and
the libraries of Deep River, Chester, New London, Groton, Mystic &
Noank.

Sandra Chalk of the New London Landmarks Society,
Jackwyn Durrschmidt, Rob Smith, president of East Haddam Land Trust;
Hazel Matey, Sue Hessel, Pamela Lithgow Briggs,
My sister, Marya Repko, for proofreading, layout and advice,
My wife, Paula, for her constant support,
interview with William Socha from the Compass – 3 april 1991
interview with David Blacker – the New London Day

The following websites:

Those of the individual landmarks plus:
lighthouse.cc;wikipedia.com; nationalregisterofhistoricplaces.com
historicbuildingsct.com, simon-pure.com, dunhamwilcox.net
cthistoryonline.org, lighthousedepot.com, bukisa.com, bridgehunter.com;
eightmileriver.org, topozone.com, mapquest.com,
newlondonlandmarks.org, nps.gov/parks

The following books:
:
the finest small museum in the country by Jackwyn Durrschmidt
Historic Glimpses by Carol Kimball
Remembering Groton by Carol Kimball
The Groton Story by Carol Kimball
Groton Revisited by Carol Kimball
Groton – Images of America Series – by Kimball, Streeter, & Comrie
Mystic – Images of America Series – by Mystic Historical Soc.
Groton 1705 – 1905 by Charles R. Stark
Lyme Yesterday by James E. Harding
Jonathan Warner 1728-1810 by Gwendolen & Harry Orton-Jones
Chester Scrap Book by Kate Silliman
The maps of Beers, Ellis, & Soule

CONTENTS

INTRODUCTION

I feel fortunate to have grown up and lived most of my life in southeastern Connecticut near the lovely Connecticut River. I now live thirty miles to the east nearby the historic Mystic River. I've always lived within ten miles of the Atlantic Ocean. I grew up before Interstate 95 was built; when two lane roads connected towns and cities; when nearly every house in my village had a barn; when the ninety-year-old woman next door refused to have indoor plumbing and drew water from her well with a rope and a bucket.

I grew up one generation too late to be educated at the one room schoolhouse just across the brook. I grew up one generation too late to wait at Hadlyme Landing for the Hartford & New York steamboat that plied the Connecticut River till the 1930's. I grew up one generation too late to build wooden boats in Noank.

But I always kept a boat on the river, down by the ferry landing. I moored her at the ramshackle pier below Gillette's castle, where William Gillette, the famous actor, had moored his one hundred forty-foot yacht. I was still a lad when the Goodspeed Opera House began restoration; still a boy when the local freight train along the river made its final passage; not quite grown when the historic Ferry Tavern in Old Lyme burned to the ground. I attended the launching of Nautilus – the world's first nuclear powered submarine – in 1954.

Local history changes in a lifetime. This booklet is an attempt to capture some of the buildings, ships, and bridges I've been familiar with. I apologize now for omitting many historic buildings. Had I made this book twice as long it would not suffice to include every historic house and tavern, mill and church in the area. Some of these buildings I've chosen have personal significance. The lighthouses are literally landmarks to those of us returning home from the sea. The theaters, museums, and restaurants are ones I frequent.

Please give me some feedback at: matthew@constantwaterman.com
Please visit my website at: www.constantwaterman.com

15 May 2010
Old Mystic, Connecticut

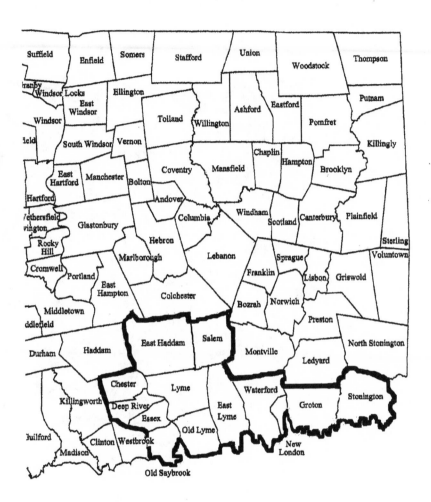

Connecticut Towns

Connecticut Department of Economic and Community Development 1996

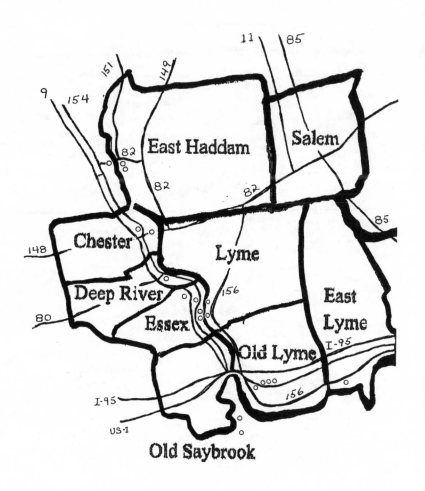

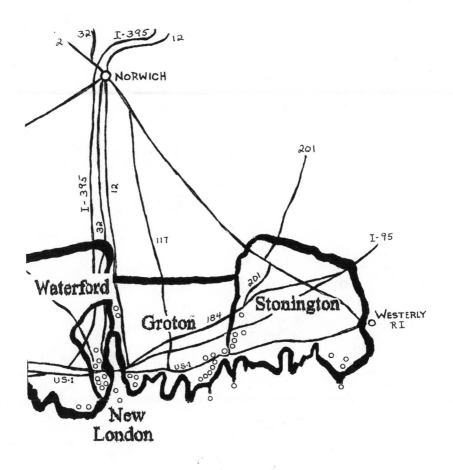

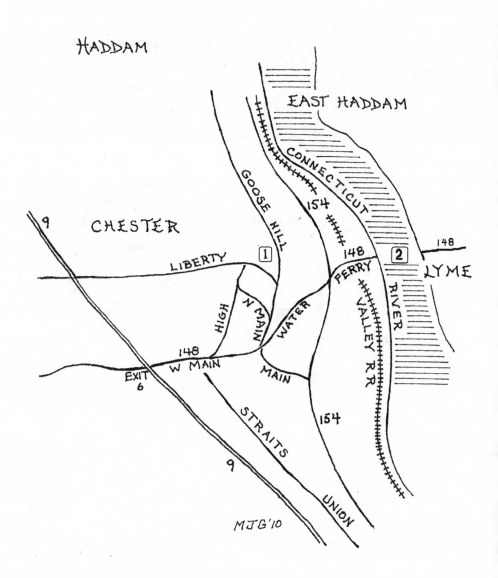

HADDAM

CHESTER

EAST HADDAM

DEEP RIVER

CHESTER

Chester Meeting House 1793

CHESTER MEETING HOUSE

4 Liberty Street, Chester, Connecticut 06412

This simple framed building stands on a small green above the bijou village of Chester. It was built in 1793 by the Ecclesiastical Society to replace an earlier meetinghouse that stood nearby and dated from 1740. This second meetinghouse served as a church from 1793 until 1845, when a third meeting house was built next to the United Church.

In 1847, the Town of Chester bought the Meeting House. For the next 113 years it housed town meetings and was known as the Old Town Hall. In 1876, a stage was added and the balcony extended. This was the renaissance of the Lower Connecticut Valley – the Goodspeed Opera House had just been built in East Haddam, a few miles away – during which performance art flourished.

The Old Town Hall served as a venue for theater, dances, recitals, and high school proms. In 1960, Chester built a new school, and most of the community functions transferred their allegiance to it. Over the following decade, the Old Town Hall hosted meetings of the Historical Society and occasional benefit programs.

In 1972, the National Register of Historic Places listed the Old Town Hall. The Historical Society decided to take action to ensure the continuance of their now famous site. Over the following year, they refurbished the building, once again known as the Chester Meeting House. Since 1973, the Meeting House has once again hosted town meetings, recitals and dramatic productions.

The Meeting House Players and The National Theatre of the Deaf perform there. The Robbie Collomore Cultural Series has hosted a variety of performers for years. Artisans and craftsman hold meetings there. Social and political organizations find the Chester Meeting House a congenial place to meet. The Meeting House is also available for weddings and private functions.

In 1985, the Historical Society built an addition behind the stage for offices and dressing rooms. An archives room was also provided to house records and memorabilia of the town of Chester.

For an application to use The Chester Meeting House, please call the Selectman's Office at 860–526–0013, extension 202. For schedules, tickets, and directions call the Meeting House at 860 –526-0015.

Selden III

CHESTER – HADLYME FERRY

Connecticut Route 148

In 1750, the Reverend Grindal Rawson, first pastor of the Hadlyme Congregational Church, was denied a permit to run a ferry to Chester from his land north of the present landing. In 1760, Samuel Selden and Simeon Church were denied a permit to operate a ferry from Selden's Landing south of today's site. Jonathan Warner of Chester [1728-1810] was granted a permit and began ferry service at this site in 1769.

In 1877, Warner's Ferry fell under the supervision of the Town of Chester and, soon after, a steam-powered barge came into service. The town renamed the service the Chester Hadlyme Ferry. In 1915, The Connecticut General Assembly assigned all river crossings to the Highway Department, who took over management of the ferry in 1917. The CT Department of Transportation currently operates this service.

Until the 1930's, Hadlyme Landing had a boat building facility and a wharf where steamboats could transfer passengers and freight. The commercialism of Hadlyme Landing resulted from the deep channel close to shore. The building closest to the ferry slip was a chandlery.

The present vessel, Selden III, is a diesel powered steel boat in service since 1949. She is 65' long, 30' wide, and carries a maximum of nine automobiles. The previous vessel, Selden II, was a three-car barge with ramps at either end, powered by a little tugboat tied alongside. After the advent of Selden III, Selden II took over service at The Rocky Hill – South Glastonbury crossing, 25 miles up river. A photo from the early 1920's shows a self-propelled vessel at Chester – perhaps the original Selden. From 1885 – 1889, the steam powered Emily Wright provided this service. A former steam vessel began to ply the river in 1879.The first ferry here was likely propelled by sweeps or poles.

In 1994, the National Register of Historic Places added the Hadlyme Ferry Historic District, including the ferry and the six venerable houses at Hadlyme Landing. For more information call 860-443-3856 or visit www.ct.gov/dot/cwp/view.asp?a=1380&Q=259724&dotPNavCtr=|4004 6|-19k

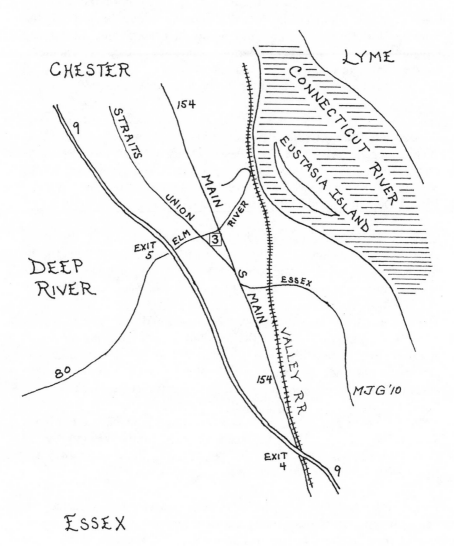

CHESTER

LYME

9

STRAITS

154

CONNECTICUT RIVER

MAIN

UNION

RIVER

EUSTASIA ISLAND

DEEP
RIVER

EXIT
5

ELM

3

S MAIN

ESSEX

80

154

VALLEY RR

MJG '10

EXIT
4

9

ESSEX

DEEP RIVER

#3 　　　　**DEEP RIVER TOWN HALL**

DEEP RIVER TOWN HALL

Corner of Elm and Main Streets, Deep River

This flatiron shaped building was designed to fit in the angle between Main Street and Elm Street – respectively Connecticut routes 9-A and 80. Previously, a hall with an auditorium owned by Charles Reed, owner of the piano factory in town and co-owner of the Pratt-Reed factory in Ivoryton, stood at this location.

The architect of the new hall was the well-known George Warren Cole of New London, project supervisor for the New London Library [page 84], Williams Memorial Institute, and the Nathan Hale School. After beginning his own business he designed the Winthrop School, the Cronin Building on State Street, New London, and a red brick flatiron edifice, the Dart Building, still to be seen on Bank Street, New London, beside the statue of Columbus. Cole died suddenly of typhoid fever during 1893 while still in his twenties.

Also of red brick, the Deep River Town Hall was completed in 1893. This handsome building housed not only the town offices but, until the 1960's, the post office as well. It also housed the Deep River Library, formed in 1900, until the library took up residence in the 1881 Richard Spencer House in 1933.

The auditorium on the third floor of the town hall, which seats 350, served for town meetings, dances, social functions, school graduations, and theatrical presentations. It currently serves as a production space for small theater companies, notably the Phoenix Theater of East Hartford and the East Haddam Stage Company.

Construction of the Town Hall came from local subscribers, who raised the $22,000 necessary. In 1905, Samuel F. Snow donated the granite fountain in front of the town hall in memory of his wife. Pratt, Reed & Company donated a Krannich and Bach piano for use in the auditorium. The Social Club purchased the stage backdrop curtains from L. J. Conch & Company in Boston.

The National Register of Historic Places listed the town hall in January 1976.

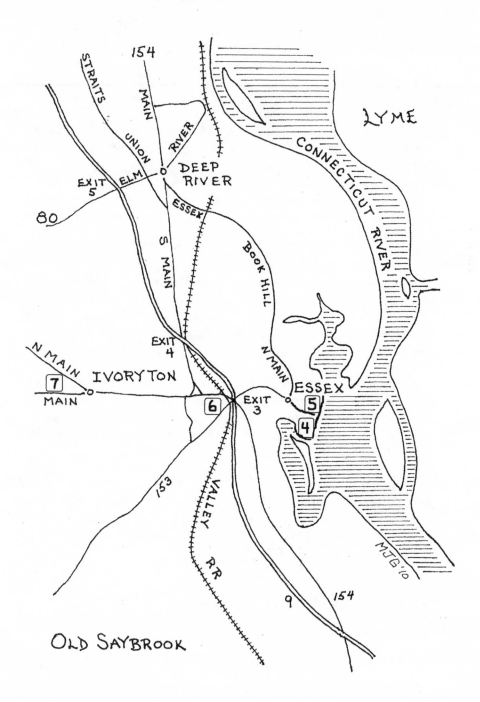

ESSEX

#4	**GRISWOLD INN**
#5	**CONNECTICUT RIVER MUSEUM**
#6	**ESSEX STEAM TRAIN**
#7	**IVORYTON PLAYHOUSE**

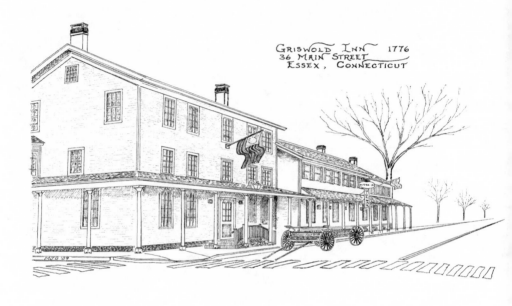

GRISWOLD INN 1776
36 MAIN STREET
ESSEX, CONNECTICUT

THE GRISWOLD INN

36 Main Street, Essex, CT 06426

The Griswold Inn, haunt of sailors beside the Connecticut River in historic Essex, is purportedly the oldest American Inn in continuous operation. Built in 1776, it was the first three-story frame structure in Connecticut. The Taproom, a former schoolhouse built in 1738, was dragged to its present location by a team of oxen. A covered bridge from New Hampshire also found a home beneath the inn's roof.

In 1814, The British burned and sank an American fleet of twenty-eight warships at Essex. They then occupied the Griswold and demanded a hunt breakfast. Every Sunday, the "Gris" still features a hunt breakfast with not only a great variety of eggs, ham, sausage, bacon, baked goods and fruits, but also venison, standing ribs, and Yorkshire pudding.

There are five dining rooms. The Library is used for the guests' complimentary continental breakfast. The Gun Room features antique firearms dating from the 15th century. The Steamboat Room has murals of local scenery. The Covered Bridge features prints by Currier and Ives.

The Taproom is a legend unto itself. Continuously voted the best bar in Connecticut by Connecticut Magazine, it has also received the praises of New York Magazine, Esquire, and others. Jazz, Dixieland, Folk, and sea shanties are all to be heard in the Taproom various evenings.

There are 31 rooms for guests all about the complex. Fourteen of these are suites; eight have fireplaces. The furniture is generally antique or reproduction Colonial. Every room has a private bath and up to date climate control. There are no TV's to be found in any room – only classical music. There is, however, a TV lounge that also has Internet hook-ups. The Inn features three eighteenth century houses on their grounds that can be reserved for conferences; convenient for groups of twelve to seventy-five.

For more information, visit their site at www.griswoldinn.com or call 860-767-1776.

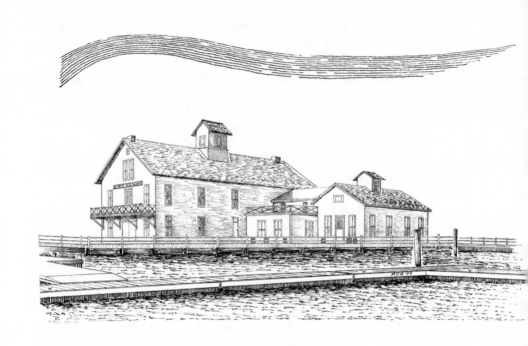

CONNECTICUT RIVER MUSEUM

67 Main Street, Essex, CT 06426

Scenic Essex, Connecticut lies on the west bank of the Connecticut River a few miles above Long Island Sound. Its Main Street ends at the river's edge. Just to your left, upstream, stands the museum. Fronting it is a sturdy wharf facing the River. This wharf and the new chandlery – 1813 - existed at the time of the British raid on Essex in 1814, when the American fleet was burned. In 1878 the warehouse was built to accommodate the steamboats that plied the river until 1931.

After its service to the steamboat trade, the "The Steamboat Dock," as the property came to be known, housed in turn a marina, a ships' store, a garage, a boat retailer, a bar, a roller rink, and a restaurant.

In 1972 the building was purchased for the Connecticut River Foundation. Funds raised from individuals and corporate sponsors underwrote the debt. The foundation, renamed the Connecticut River Museum, became a part of the state's bicentennial project. Restoration of the warehouse and chandlery got underway. Governor Ella Grasso became the first paid member and ex officio patron. Since then there have been 125 trustees emeriti and over 1200 members. The National Register of Historic Places listed the Steamboat Dock in 1982.

In 1975, the chandlery opened its doors. Thomas A. Stevens, a former director of Mystic Seaport, donated his nautical library. In May of 1982 the renovated warehouse opened. The Wadsworth Atheneum in Hartford loaned the museum a collection of nautical artifacts and artwork. In 1989, a 800 square foot boathouse was added to display ship models and a replica of the 1776 submarine Turtle, designed by David Bushnell for use against British ships.

The museum operates the 54' *RiverQuest*, a twin hulled tour boat that conducts year round excursions of the lower river, sunset cruises during the summer, and eagle sightings in February. For more information on the museum and *RiverQuest*, visit them at www.ctrivermuseum.org or call 860 – 767 – 8269.

29

ESSEX STEAM TRAIN

One Railroad Avenue, Essex, Connecticut 06426

In 1868, the State of Connecticut granted a charter to James C. Walkeley to build a railroad from Old Saybrook to Hartford along the west bank of the Connecticut River. On 29 July 1871, the first train ran the 45-mile route. The schedule specified four round trips per day [except Sundays] of passenger service, and one that would carry passengers and freight. In 1876, the Connecticut Valley Railroad defaulted on its mortgage. In 1880, the Hartford and Connecticut Valley Railroad took them over. Two years later, they sold the Valley Line to the New Haven Railroad. The New Haven maintained and improved the Valley RR, but after World War I, the increased use of cars and trucks encroached on the railroad business. The Valley RR kept decreasing service until, during the 1950's, when I was a boy, it ran but two freights a day. In 1961, the New Haven RR declared itself bankrupt. Valley RR decreased its runs to two freights per week. In 1968, the New Haven RR went out of business. The last run of the Valley RR was in March 1968.

When Penn Central took over the railroad, they slated the Valley RR for demolition. A volunteer group convinced Penn Central to give the Valley RR to the State. Connecticut granted a lease to the newly found Valley RR Company in 1970, allowing the use of 22.67 miles of track. After much fund raising and work, done mostly by volunteers, the Valley Railroad Company celebrated its first run from Essex to Deep River on 29 July 1971 – 100 years to the day from the initial ceremony.

The Essex Steam Train draws old coaches from Essex to Haddam Landing. Some runs exchange passengers with the paddle wheel tour boat, Becky Thatcher. This is the only steam train and riverboat cruise in the country. Numerous special programs include: a Thomas the Tank Engine outing; a scary Halloween ride; the Santa Claus Special; the North Pole Express; the Murder Mystery run; and the luxurious Essex Clipper Dinner Train. Pictured here is an ALCO/Cooke type 2-8-0 locomotive, built in 1923.

River Valley Junction includes Essex Depot; the Display Building; and the Oliver O. Jensen Gallery. Books, artwork, and gifts are available. For yearly schedules, programs, blog, tickets & directions, go to www.essexsteamtrain.com or call: 800-377-3987 or 860-767-0103.

IVORYTON PLAYHOUSE

103 Main Street, Ivoryton, Connecticut 06442

In 1911, the Comstock-Cheney factory built the playhouse as a recreation hall for its employees. Ivoryton was widely known for processing ninety percent of all the ivory imported by America. Comstock-Cheney produced buttons, billiard balls, and piano keys.

Milton Stiefel began his career as an actor. He ended up backstage as assistant director to the great David Belasco. After the demise of Belasco, Stiefel went on to direct many productions around the country. Recuperating in scenic Essex, Connecticut, he found the now unused recreation hall and saw it as a venue for a resident stock company.

"Broken Dishes," featuring brand new actress Bette Davis, had just closed in New York. It opened in Ivoryton in June of 1930. Stiefel's company, known as "The New York Players," stayed in private homes in Ivoryton during the season. By 1938, Stiefel bought the theater and continued to make it not only a going concern, but also a showcase for some of the biggest stars in theater.

Henry Hull and Norma Terrace, already established, performed there. Burgeoning actors Kate Hepburn and Cliff Robertson made a name there. Though the playhouse shut down during the dark days of World War II, Stiefel reopened it after the war. A formidable array of stars from Broadway and Hollywood found their way to Ivoryton: Marlon Brando, Art Carney, Ethel Waters, Talullah Bankhead, Groucho Marx, June Lockhart, Betty Grable, Ezio Pinza, and Don Ameche.

Stiefel retired in 1973 and sold the Ivoryton Playhouse to Ken Krezel. Krezel had little luck with it and sold it to the Ivoryton Playhouse Foundation in 1979. The Foundation enjoyed little luck. In 1987, The River Rep took it over and it became an instant success.

Over the next 28 years, the playhouse enjoyed a complete renovation, thanks in part to grants from the state of Connecticut. As of 2006 the Foundation began to produce plays all year round.

Please visit: www.ivorytonplayhouse.org or call 860-767-7318.

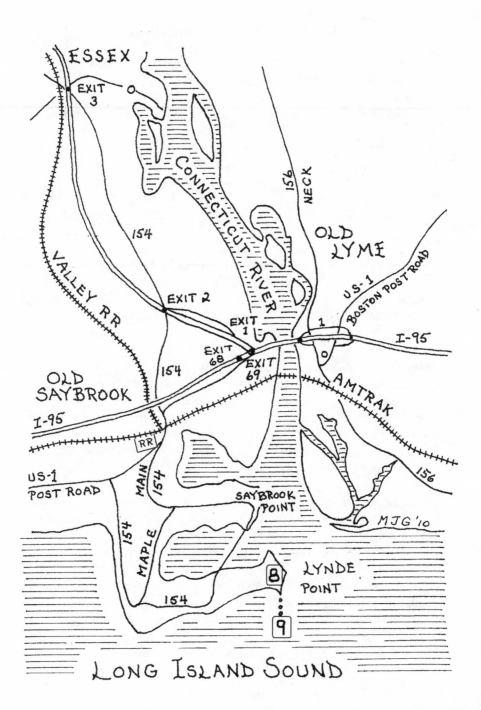

ESSEX

EXIT 3

CONNECTICUT RIVER

154

NECK

156

OLD LYME

US-1 BOSTON POST ROAD

VALLEY RR

EXIT 2

EXIT 1

EXIT 68

EXIT 69

1

1

I-95

OLD SAYBROOK

154

AMTRAK

I-95

156

RR

US-1 POST ROAD

MAIN

154

MAPLE

154

SAYBROOK POINT

MJG '10

154

LYNDE POINT

8

9

LONG ISLAND SOUND

34

OLD SAYBROOK

LYNDE POINT LIGHTHOUSE

Lynde Point, Old Saybrook, Connecticut 06475

41° 16.28' North, 72° 20.60' West

Abisha Woodward of New London, who built the New London Harbor Light in 1801, constructed a 35' wooden light beacon on Lynde Point in 1803. It proved too short to afford sufficient visibility. In 1838, a 65' octagonal, brownstone tower similar to the New London Harbor Light [see page 92] was built. It had a wooden spiral staircase, replaced in 1868. Its radiance consisted of 10 lamps with reflectors. In 1852, these were replaced with a fourth-order Fresnel lens. This was downgraded to a fifth-order Fresnel in 1890. A bell was installed in 1854.

The light keeper's cottage was used from 1833 till 1858, then replaced by a Gothic Revival house. The Coast Guard removed this in 1966 and, contrary to the inclinations of the Saybrook Historical Society, replaced it with a modern duplex.

Shifting sandbars have always plagued the mouth of the Connecticut. In 1875, a jetty that jutted into Long Island Sound was constructed along the west bank, just below Lynde Point. Five years later, a parallel jetty was built in the river. The dredged channel between them assures constant access. When The Breakwater Light [page 38] was built in 1886, it was often referred to as the "Outer Light," while the one at Lynde Point became known as the "Inner Light." The two are about a mile and a half apart apart.

Lynde Point Light was electrified in 1955 and automated in 1978. The lighthouse is still an active aid to navigation and displays a fixed white light. The road to it is closed to the public and the lighthouse is best viewed from the water.

The National Register of Historic Places listed Lynde Point Light in 1990. To find out all about this and other Connecticut lighthouses, read Jeremy D'Entremont's book, *The Lighthouses of Connecticut*. For information on lighthouses of New York and New England, visit his extensive website, to which I am greatly indebted, at www.lighthouse.cc

JETTY LIGHT
OLD SAYBROOK
CONNECTICUT

BREAKWATER LIGHTHOUSE

Old Saybrook, Connecticut

41° 15.79' North, 72° 20.57 West

A huge and shifting sandbar has always obstructed access to the mouth of the Connecticut River. Between 1875 and 1880, twin jetties were constructed and the channel between was kept dredged. Two miles beyond, bell number eight gives the mariner a course to steer amid Long Sand Shoals.

Lynde Point Light, the Inner Light, [see page 36] was constructed in 1838. The Breakwater Light, or Outer Light, was constructed in 1886. It's a 49' cast iron tower lined with brick, with a focal plane of 58'. Four stories high, its lantern room was fitted with a fifth order Fresnel lens. In 1890, a fourth order lens was installed. In 1889, a 1000-pound bell was installed, but at the insistence of the residents, replaced with one of only 250 pounds. Later a foghorn was installed. In 1936, two diaphragm horns ensured a distinct signal.

On September 21, 1938, the most severe hurricane in at least a generation devastated Long Island and the shores of southern New England. The lightship at New London dragged her massive anchors and ended on a sandbar two miles farther east. The Breakwater Light at Old Saybrook withstood the hurricane. Her fuel tanks were carried away; the jetty suffered damage; but the stalwart little lighthouse stood the strain. When the engine room was flooded, keepers Gross and Bennett switched to the oil lamp.

In 1959, the lamp was automated and modernized. In 2007, the light was offered to private ownership under the National Historic Lighthouse Preservation Act of 2000. It presently seems to be in limbo; the Coast Guard insisting its light and horn be maintained as a notice to mariners. Its signal is a fixed white light punctuated by a flashing green light every six seconds. A fixed red sector warns mariners of a dangerous approach.

For more information read Jeremy D'Entremont's book *The Lighthouses of Connecticut*. For information on New England lighthouses visit his extensive website, to which I am greatly indebted, at www,lighthouse.cc

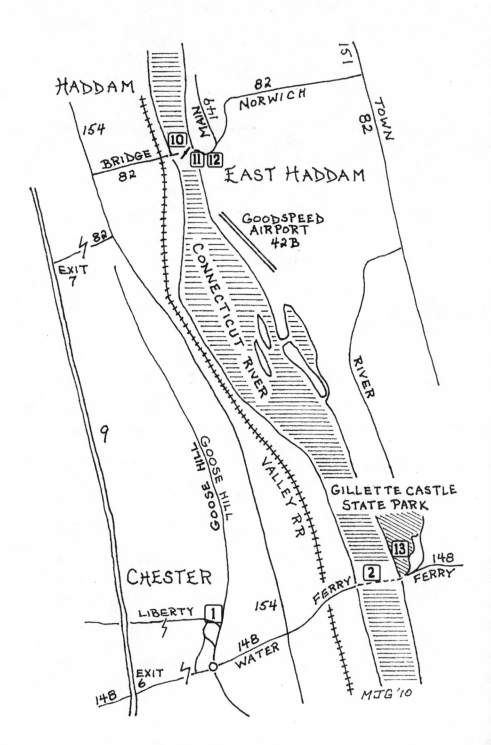

HADDAM

154

BRIDGE
82

EXIT
7

82

9

CHESTER

LIBERTY

EXIT
6

148

82
NORWICH

151

TOWN

82

MAIN 149

10

11 12

EAST HADDAM

GOODSPEED
AIRPORT
42B

CONNECTICUT RIVER

RIVER

GOOSE HILL

VALLEY RR

GILLETTE CASTLE
STATE PARK

13

148
FERRY

2

FERRY

1

154

148
WATER

MJG '10

EAST HADDAM

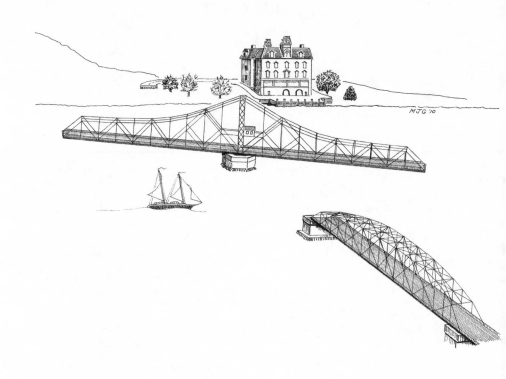

42

42

EAST HADDAM SWING BRIDGE

Connecticut Route 82

This steel, swing truss bridge crosses the Connecticut River 14 miles north of Long Island Sound. It connects the towns of Haddam and East Haddam via CT route 82 and currently averages 11,600 vehicles per day. It is listed at the National Historic Register of Places, www.nps.org, www.bukisa.com/worlds-most-notable-bridges; www.bridgehunter.com

It was designed by Alfred P. Boller [1840–1912] and fabricated by the American Bridge Company. From its opening on 14 June 1913 until 2001, its swing span of 456' was the longest in the world. In 2001, El Ferdan Railway Bridge, with a span of 340 meters [1115'] was constructed across the Suez Canal. The East Haddam Bridge includes three spans totaling 881'. The swing span, originating on the East Haddam bank, has a center-bearing pivot and moving-wedge end lifts. The adjacent Pennsylvania Truss fixed span is 326'. There is a short approach span from the Haddam shore.

Haddam Landing on the west bank was important for its railroad. The small station by the bridge served the Connecticut Valley RR Company, and its successor, the New Haven RR Company, that maintained a line from Old Saybrook to Hartford from 1871 until 1968. The Landing is now the terminus of the Essex Steam Train [page 30].

Previous to the current bridge, a ferry connected Haddam and East Haddam. The first charter from the Colonial government of Middlesex County, to Captain John Chapman in May of 1694 grants: "...the privilege of setting up a ferry over the Great River in Haddam..." By the end of the 19th century, this ferry belonged to one of the Goodspeeds. As thick ice during the winters precluded ferry traffic, and the volume of motorized traffic increased, a bridge became a necessity.

At present, the nearest bridges are the Baldwin Bridge between Old Lyme and Old Saybrook, twelve miles to the south at the river mouth, and the Aragoni Bridge, about fourteen miles up river between Middletown and Portland. The Chester-Hadlyme Ferry [page 18], three miles downstream, carries but nine cars, has a weight limit of 5 tons, and runs but eight months a year.

GELSTON HOUSE RESTAURANT

8 Main Street, East Haddam, Connecticut 06423

In 1736, Jabez Chapman was licensed to run a tavern where the Gelston House now stands. He named it the Riverside Inn. In 1773, William Gelston purchased the establishment. In 1783, Uriah Rogers built a new tavern. In 1826, it changed hands again. The new buyer was Joseph Goodspeed, father of the William H. Goodspeed who, fifty years later, would build the Goodspeed Opera House [page 44] next door. Under management of Solomon Belden, the premises were known as Beldon's Hotel. In 1853, The Gelston Hotel Company formed. It included Joseph's sons, William & George Goodspeed, and was headed by George & Hugh Gelston, sons of William. They erected a new building on the site, incorporating Rogers' tavern as part of it. Known as the Gelston House, it also housed the Bank of New England. In 1865, William Goodspeed purchased the hotel, and the bank reorganized as The National Bank of New England, which remained on the premises another century.

After William H. Goodspeed's death in 1882, his son, William Robbins Goodspeed, took over. In 1888, he sold to Nolan Newberry. Two years later, it became the property of former manager, Ralph Swan, and kept the name of Hotel Swan till 1909. In that year Edwin Rose bought it and changed the name back to the Riverside Inn. For 85 years it kept that name, though it changed ownership often and went in and out of business. In 1994, the Goodspeed Opera House Foundation purchased it and changed the name back to The Gelston House.

Cuisine at the Gelston House is a blend of American and Continental. The River Grill Restaurant is the formal dining room and fronts the Connecticut River. The Gelston Tavern is the more informal area. The Beer Garden is outside, at the rear of the building, and has a magnificent view of the river valley. There is a Prix Fixe selection for theatergoers, and a late night menu for diners after the show. Cabaret, Jazz, or the Blues are offered on Friday and Saturday evenings, and brunch is offered on Sundays. The Gelston House has seating for 125 and maintains six guest rooms, plus rooms for conferences and private parties. Visit them at www.gelstonhouse.com or call 860-873-1411.

The National Register of Historic Places has listed the Gelston House in East Haddam's historic district number one.

GILLETTE'S CASTLE – "THE SEVENTH SISTER" - 1919

67 River Road, East Haddam, CT 06423

William Hooker Gillette, 1853-1937, was born in Hartford. His lifetime in the theater was marked by resounding success. Known mostly today for his vivid portrayal of Arthur Conan Doyle's *Sherlock Holmes*, Gillette was known in his own day for the realism and suspense of his own plays, notably those of the Civil War, *Held by the Enemy* [1886] and *Secret Service* [1896]. Without bias towards either North or South, he chose to portray characters as mixtures of good and evil; to make his plays realistic in the age of melodrama; to create true to life scenery and lighting and sound effects. Gillette wrote 13 plays; collaborated on 7 others; and acted in his own plays as well as those of other notable playwrights such as James Barrie. Between 1899 and 1932 - at age 79, he performed as Sherlock Holmes in 1300 productions. He acted in New York, London, and on tours, earning the admiration and applause of theatergoers. He amassed a fortune.

Between Goodspeed's Landing and Hadlyme Landing, along the east bank of the lower Connecticut River, stand seven low hills – the Seven Sisters. Cruising up the Connecticut aboard his 144' houseboat, *Aunt Polly*, Gillette saw the house site he'd always wanted: a steep hill with a superb view of the river. He bought 184 acres and designed a chateau on the lines of a Norman Castle.

Built of local fieldstone over a steel framework, *The Seventh Sister* has 24 rooms, the largest the 30' by 50' living room with its massive fireplace. The interiors are of white oak panels, with 47 unique, massive oak doors with hidden latches. There are built-in cabinets, a solarium, and a frog pond. Outside, a broad terrace overlooks the Connecticut, 200 feet below. An avid admirer of the railroad, Gillette installed over three miles of 17-gauge track for his miniature train. The grounds of *The Seventh Sister* have numerous walking trails, goldfish and lily ponds, and stunning views of the river.

After Gillette died, his property was sold to the State of Connecticut. It became Gillette Castle State Park in 1943. The National Register of Historic Places listed it in 1986. Please visit: www.stateparks.com/gillette_castle.html or call 866-287–2757 or 860–526–2336.

EIGHT MILE RIVER WATERSHED

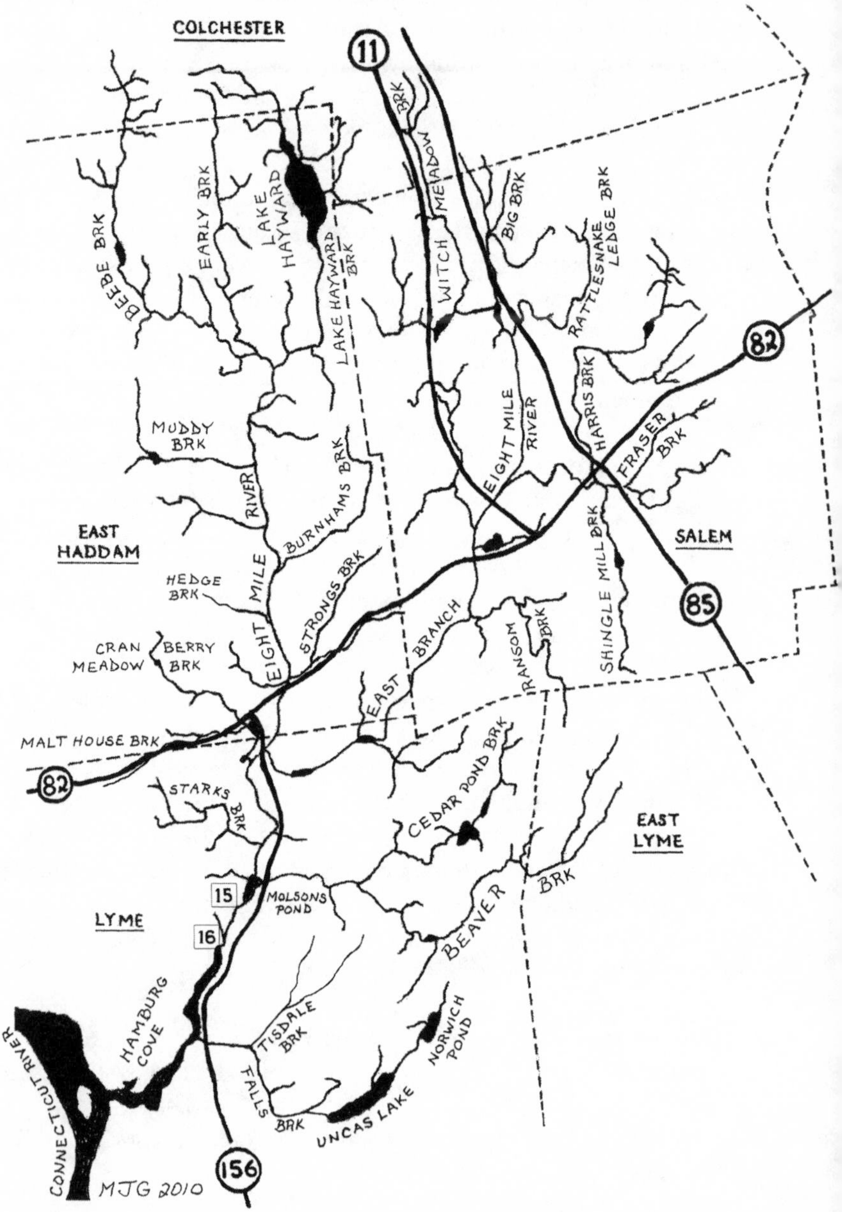

COLCHESTER

BEEBE BRK

EARLY BRK

LAKE HAYWARD

LAKE HAYWARD BRK

WITCH MEADOW BRK

BIG BRK

RATTLESNAKE LEDGE BRK

11

82

MUDDY BRK

BURNHAMS BRK

EIGHT MILE RIVER

HARRIS BRK

FRASER BRK

EAST HADDAM

HEDGE BRK

STRONGS BRK

EIGHT MILE RIVER

SHINGLE MILL BRK

SALEM

CRAN MEADOW

BERRY BRK

EAST BRANCH

RANSOM BRK

85

MALT HOUSE BRK

82

STARKS BRK

CEDAR POND BRK

EAST LYME

LYME

15

16

MOLSONS POND

BEAVER BRK

HAMBURG COVE

TISDALE BRK

NORWICH POND

CONNECTICUT RIVER

FALLS BRK

UNCAS LAKE

MJG 2010

156

48

LYME

EIGHT MILE RIVER WATERSHED

#14   **OSPREY**
#15   **RED MILL**
#16   **OLD HAMBURG BRIDGE**

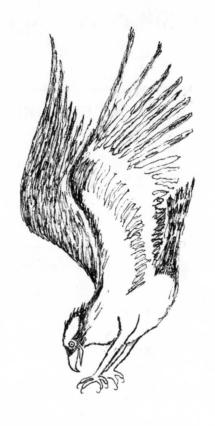

EIGHT MILE RIVER

www.eightmileriver.org

Although Eight Mile River begins just above Devil's Hopyard State Park in East Haddam, three brooks converge to form it: Lake Hayward Brook - in the northeast corner of East Haddam; Beebe Brook, or North Book, now often designated the Eight Mile River, and Tanyard Brook [Early Brook]. The East Branch of the Eight Mile River flows out of Salem; the two converge just where East Haddam borders on the town of Lyme. The numerous tributaries had sufficient waterpower to run small mills, though often no more than a few months out of the year.

At various times and locations during the eighteenth and nineteenth centuries, Beebe Brook powered four different sawmills and a gristmill. Tanyard Brook powered at least one sawmill as well as a tannery, and perhaps a fulling mill. A sawmill and a gristmill stood just by the outfall of Lake Hayward. Above Chapman Falls, two sawmills and a gristmill were powered by Eight Mile River. During the nineteenth century, the Chapman house stood between the twin outfalls of a millpond. On the west side was a gristmill; on the east, a sawmill. Below, the streams converged before plunging sixty feet at a steep cascade still known as Chapman Falls. I'm told that the slabs from the sawmill were tossed into the river to go over the falls. The Chapman sawmill, rebuilt by Mr. Babcock, remained in operation till 1908. Another sawmill, on Beebe Brook, originally owned by an earlier Chapman, continued to be used till the 1930's. This mill eventually exchanged its up-and-down saw for a circular saw, then had a gang of circular saws for ripping planks for ships. Both the upper and lower landings at East Haddam, only a few miles away, had busy shipbuilding facilities.

There were also mills at Jones Hill Road and West Dolbia Hill Road just below the Hopyard. From the west, Muddy Brook enters from nearby Will Cone Pond. Downstream Burnhams Brook and Strongs Brook enter from the East; Hedge Brook from the west. Another stream entering from the west took the name of Malthouse Brook from the brewing business that flourished there before1814. Cranberry Meadow Brook swells Malthouse Brook from the north. Before Malthouse Brook joins Eight Mile River in the town of Lyme, it once powered a little mill used to clean clover seed.

51

Almost immediately, the East Branch joins it, flowing from the town of Salem. The East Branch is fed by Witch Meadow Brook with its pond just south of Witch Meadow Road in Salem; by Big Brook, which crosses Witch Meadow Road where there's a pond just north of the road; and by Rattlesnake Ledge Brook. Farther downstream, Harris Brook, that begins at Salem Four Corners, and is fed by Fowlers Brook and Shingle Mill Brook, flows into the East Branch. A tiny stream that flows through Mitchell Pond on the Bingham Estate joins the Branch just to the south. Ransom Brook then enters from the east. Thence the East Branch flows through Wagner Pond, where Beck's Sawmill once stood, thence into Ed Bill's Pond. This large pond, just upstream from the confluence of the Branch with the Eight Mile River, has a fish ladder and pipe built into its dam to allow salmon, trout, shad, and alewives to ascend and spawn.

As Eight Mile River meanders into Lyme, it passes through two more ponds. Just downstream, Stark's Brook enters from the west. Then comes a shallow pond with a sandy beach and picnic area used by local residents. Less than a mile downstream spreads Molson Pond. Beaver Brook flows into it from the east. There are several millponds upstream, most notably Blackwell's Pond. Cedar Pond Brook, which joins Beaver Brook, passes through Cedar Lake and E. A. Whitford Pond. In the 18th century, Lee's sawmill stood above Cedar Pond.

Just below Molson Pond, off Mount Archer Road, stands an old mill, pictured here – possibly the only water mill standing in the entire watershed. A fish ladder and pipe ascend the tailrace that runs beneath the building. The mill can be viewed from the bridge, as it looks here. Locally referred to as the Red Mill, this structure dates from 1785. In 1680, the town granted the right to build a sawmill to Richard Lord, Joseph Peck, and Edward Woolfe. By 1727 it was referred to as The Eight Mile River Mill. A site map dated 1739 names this site Marvin's Mills. By the 1750's, Duncan McIntosh operated a gristmill, known as the McIntosh Mill, at this site. In 1784, a flood destroyed this facility. In 1785, the present mill was erected by Samuel Gibbs and Abner Griffing, the heirs of Duncan McIntosh. By 1845, a joint stock company had conceived the Hamburgh [sic] Mfg Company, to work with textiles. The next conveyance, in 1857, to an Albert Rathbun, mentions a dye house. The millpond is sometimes referred to as Rathbun's Pond. The next conveyance, in 1910, mentions a factory and a sawmill. A conveyance in 1940 mentions two dwellings and two factory buildings. In 1946, the mill became the site of Red Mill Weavers,

John Delle Donne, President. By the next conveyance, in 1954, no mention of commercial use is mentioned, though from 1983 till 1990, Red Mill, Inc. owned the building. Since 1990 it has been a private residence, the deed demanding the maintenance of Rathbun Dam and the raceway.

A mile more and the river passes beneath a lovely arched bridge on Mount Archer Road, following which it slows and spreads, and becomes the uppermost reach of Hamburg Cove. On either bank stand proud Colonial and Federal homes with small but well kempt lawns. This area just below the bridge was known as Reed's Landing – later as Old Hamburg - and the river was dredged from here to Hamburg Cove. From 1710–1776, the Sterling Shipyard built vessels here. During the early nineteenth century, lumber was shipped. A painting by G. F. Bottume from the mid eighteen hundreds depicts a bustling hamlet. The present bridge, depicted here, replaced the previous one of stone and timber that was washed away in the flood of 1936. In 1983, The National Register of Historic Places listed Reed's Landing as a historic district. A half-mile farther, Hamburg Cove supports a pair of marinas. A sizeable estuary a mile long connects it to the Connecticut River. The village of Hamburg, a part of Lyme, perches above the cove.

Lastly, Falls Brook, fed by Tisdale Brook, flows into the head of Hamburg Cove. This brook connects to sizeable Uncas Lake – known during the 1700's as Hog Pond - and Norwich Pond. Both now lie within Nehantic State Forest. Tisdale Brook once had a tannery and a fulling mill and was known as Fulling Mill Brook. Falls Brook had a large natural waterfall. The town conceded the right to build and operate a gristmill and sawmill with milling rates fixed by the town. William Sterling, who ran the shipyard at Reed's Landing, took up the concession and sawed wood for his boats. A channel was built downstream to bring up logs and take away milled lumber.

The more than 20 brooks that feed the Eight Mile River watershed drain approximately 60 square miles. They comprise 161 miles of watercourses. There probably are, or were, about 30 ponds that powered water mills. Today, most of the mills are gone and many dams ruined. Occasionally, an old flume can be found beside a brook. On 8 May 2008, President George Bush approved a bill conferring "wild and scenic waterway" status to Eight Mile River. Under the "Partnership Rivers" program, the National Park Service now protects and manages Eight Mile River.

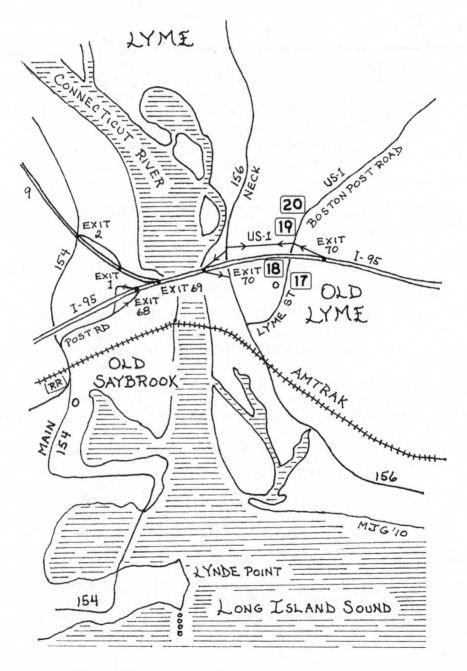

OLD LYME

#17	**PHOEBE GRIFFIN NOYES LIBRARY**
#18	**LYME ACADEMY**
#19	**LYME ART ASSOCIATION**
#20	**FLORENCE GRISWOLD HOUSE**

PHOEBE GRIFFIN NOYES LIBRARY   1898

MJG 09

58

PHOEBE GRIFFIN NOYES LIBRARY

2 Library Lane, Old Lyme, CT 06371

Phoebe Griffin grew up in the Lord House on the site of the present library. Her family supported her while she continued her studies. Afterwards, she returned to Old Lyme and married Daniel Noyes, who had a general store on Lyme Street. They bought a house next door to the Congregational Church where Phoebe taught village children for thirty years. She had six children. A daughter, Josephine, married a wealthy businessman from New York, Charles H. Luddington. They spent their summers in Old Lyme, then built a house there and settled. Luddington donated the funds to build the library and dedicated it to his mother-in-law. Built in 1897, it opened its doors 23 June 1898.

The Ladies Library Association, which for many years managed the library, helped raise funds for the building by hanging and selling local paintings. As the Old Lyme Colony at the Florence Griswold House just up the road had its inception concurrent with the opening of the Noyes, plenty of paintings of merit became available. From 1902 till the completion of their gallery in 1921, The Lyme Art Colony – later the Lyme Art Association [page 62] – held summertime exhibitions at the library. By 1913, the Town of Old Lyme began to fund the library.

In 1924, the library added the MacCurdy-Salisbury Wing. In 1938, they added a children's wing. In 1960 they completed another addition. In 1995, they opened another, effectively doubling the library's space.

In 1970, the Ladies Library Association merged with the Phoebe Griffin Noyes Trust to become the Old Lyme-Phoebe Griffin Noyes Library Association. In 1986, the library joined Lion, Inc – the computerized library network. The library now boasts numerous computers and a community meeting room. The library is presently ADA compliant to serve more people. The enthusiastic Friends of the Library manage Phoebe's Book Cellar Shop to sell used books. Free or discounted passes to local art and natural history museums as well as the aquarium and the zoo are available on request to holders of a Connecticut library card.

The Noyes Library also hosts the Connecticut River Film Forum, Phoebe's Book Chat, small art shows, lectures, readings, JobNow workshops, and a writers' workshop. Visit them at www.olpgnlib.org , www.oldlyme.lioninc.org , or call 860-434-1684.

ACADEMY of FINE ARTS

84 Lyme Street, Old Lyme, CT 06371

Founded in 1976 by Elisabeth Gordon Chandler, Lyme Academy now has an enrollment 150 - 96 undergraduates and 54 continuing their studies. A BFA is offered in painting, sculpting, and illustrating. Only half the student body is from Connecticut. The student to faculty ratio is only fourteen to one. The arts library has 13,000 volumes, 70 periodicals, 24,000 slides, and numerous CD's.

This small campus is situated on 47 acres overlooking the picturesque Lieutenant River in the Colonial village of Old Lyme. It is only an hour from Hartford or New Haven; only two hours from Boston or New York City.

In the late eighteen hundreds, Old Lyme became a center for impressionism, thanks greatly to Florence Griswold, whose home became a haven for artists looking to capture the ambiance of the lower Connecticut River, its salt marshes and meadows. The Florence Griswold House [page 64], the Griswold Museum, and the Lyme Art Association [page 62] are nearly next door to the Academy. The main street of Old Lyme is lined with galleries of fine art, stately Colonial houses, and noteworthy restaurants.

Lyme Academy is accredited by the New England Association of Schools and Colleges [NEASC], the National Association of Schools of Art and Design [NASAD], and the Connecticut Department of Higher Education.

Please visit them at: www.lymeacademy.edu or call them at 860-434-8032

LYME ART ASSOCIATION

90 Lyme Street, Old Lyme, CT 06371

At the end of the nineteenth century, Impressionist painters discovered the town of Old Lyme. A sleepy village at the mouth of the lovely Connecticut River, it offered vistas of estuaries, salt marshes, tumbling brooks, Colonial houses, a stately church, fields, cattle, farms, and the river itself, with its sailboats and numerous coves and wharves. As with most Impressionists, their major goal was the interpretation of light, but the American school tended to be more representational than that of most Europeans.

These early artists also discovered Miss Florence Griswold, who extended them her hospitality. Gifford Beal, Willard Metcalf, Will Howe Foote, Henry Rankin Poore, Childe Hassam, and William Chadwick were some of the notables who, in 1914, formed the Lyme Art Association. They had held exhibitions at the Noyes Library [page 58] every summer since 1902. But they needed a gallery of their own.

In 1917, they purchased some land from Florence Griswold adjacent to her house. Artist Lawton Parker became chairman of the building committee. It retained the services of architect Charles Platt, designer of the Freer Art Gallery in Washington, D. C. and the Lyman Allyn Museum in New London [page 80].

The resultant building was praised by the New York Times as "an embodiment of art in harmony with its natural surroundings." It opened on 6 August 1921. In 1938, Mrs. William Owen Goodman funded a fourth room, the Goodman Gallery, in memory of her husband, the Association's third president. The National Register of Historic Places added the gallery to its list in 1986.

The Association hosts their Annual Summer Exhibition, as well as other shows featuring new or regional artists. All shows are juried. In 1938, they first allowed other mediums beside oil paints and sculpture. In 1992, the Association held their first Annual Associate Members' Exhibition. The mission of the Lyme Art Association is, and has been, to promote representational art; to encourage local artists; and to both preserve and sell fine works of art. Visit them at: www.lymeartassociation.org or call: 860-434-7802.

Florence Griswold House 1817

FLORENCE GRISWOLD HOUSE - 1817

96 Lyme Street, Old Lyme, CT 06371

Florence Griswold [1850–1937] was a resident of Old Lyme. After teaching for fourteen years, circumstances forced her to take borders into her home to make a living. Beginning in 1899, artists, attracted by the vistas available, began to rent rooms from her. They encouraged their friends to come and stay and paint. Inspired by the French Barbizon School, American Impressionism found a home in Old Lyme. The Lyme Art Colony was launched.

Henry Ward Ranger, Childe Hassam, William Metcalf, Lydia and Breta Longacre were among the earliest members of this colony of artists. Later, Matilda Browne and William Chadwick would compliment them. The first wife of President Wilson, Ellen Louise Wilson, came to Florence Griswold as a student. President Wilson and his family would come to stay over several years.

Four years after the Lyme Art Association [page 62] formed in 1914, Florence donated the land adjacent to her home to build their gallery. She became their first manager in 1921 when the gallery opened. In 1936, Miss Florence sold her house and land to Judge Robert McCurdy Marsh, who gave her life tenancy until her death a year later. In 1941, the Florence Griswold Association purchased her house. In 1947, it first opened its doors as an art museum.

In 1955, the Florence Griswold Association became a part of the Lyme Historical Society. By 1972, the museum hired a full time, professional director; in 1979, a full time curator. By 1980, the museum's exhibitions and collections had won it national recognition. Over the years, collections of art, purchased or donated, enriched the museum till the Florence Griswold House needed to expand. In 1993, The National Register of Historic Places designated the Florence Griswold House a National Historic Landmark.

Having acquired some of the original acreage fronting the Lieutenant River, the Museum built the Robert and Nancy Krieble Gallery. This 10,000 square foot addition added gallery space, storage, offices, and a gift shop. The Florence Griswold House, maintained in the fashion of 1910, features fine art, ceramics, toys and dolls, furniture, textiles, and historic artifacts, as well as the archives of the Lyme Historical Society. Please visit them at: www.flogris.org or call 860-434-542.

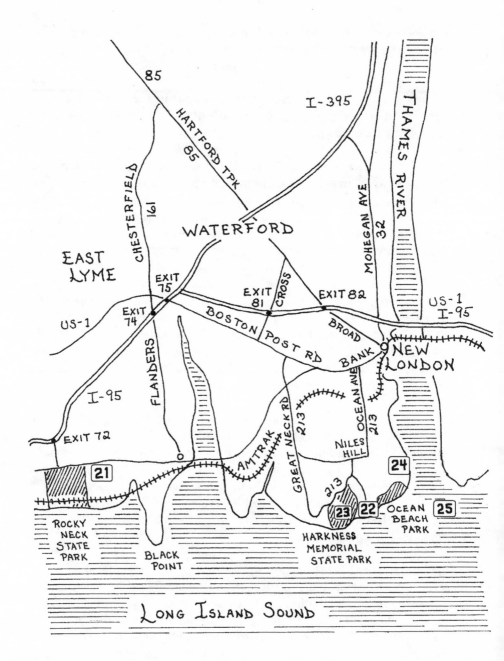

EAST LYME, WATERFORD, & NEW LONDON HARBOR

#21	**THOMAS LEE HOUSE**
#22	**O'NEILL THEATER CENTER**
#23	**HARKNESS MANSION**
#24	**HARBOR LIGHTHOUSE**
#25	**LEDGE LIGHTHOUSE**

THOMAS LEE HOUSE – circa 1660

228 West Main Street [rt. 156], East Lyme, Connecticut 06333

Thomas Lee II [1639-1704] came to America from Sussex, England with his parents, Thomas Lee and Phoebe Brown Lee, and two sisters, Jane and Sarah, at the age of 6. After the death of his father, the family came to Old Saybrook. Young Thomas found a friend in Mr. Matthew Griswold of Lyme, who cared for him and granted him a parcel of land. Thomas continued to acquire property all his life and became wealthy and influential. He served as a deputy, land recorder, assessor, surveyor, rate collector, examiner of weights and measures, and was an Ensign in the militia. In 1670 he married Sarah Kirtland of Lynn, Massachusetts and they settled into their new house. Sarah died in 1676, leaving three children. Thomas' second wife, Marah DeWolfe, bore him eleven children. After Ensign Lee's death, the house went to his son, Thomas Lee III, and, on his death in 1752, to his grandson Elisha.

The house is a typical post and beam structure of saltbox design – two stories in front but one story in back; the back pitch of the roof considerably longer than the front pitch. A huge fireplace covered most of the west wall. About 1700 an addition was built onto the west wall. About 1765, another addition was built. There is a barn on the property, plus The Little Boston Schoolhouse, 1805, which was moved to the property. This one room school was active in East Lyme until 1922. The barn has exhibits and artifacts concerning the Colonists and Nehantic Tribe. A store sells reproductions of Colonial games, books and cards.

The Lee House and schoolhouse have been kept as period pieces. The National Register of Historic Places added the Thomas Lee House in 1970. Now under the auspices of the East Lyme Historical Society, The Lee House also dispenses current information about the surrounding area. The property is open only during the summer. Guided tours of the three buildings and the old fashioned garden are available.

For more information call: 860-739-6070 or visit: www.eastlymehistoricalsociety.org

EUGENE O'NEILL THEATER CENTER

305 Great Neck Road, Waterford, Connecticut 06385

The Eugene O'Neill Theater Center was the dream child of George C. White, a local Waterford resident. In 1961, the town of Waterford purchased the seaside Hammond farm of ninety-five acres at 305 Great Neck Road. The plan to burn the old farmhouse, barn, and outbuildings to be rid of them was halted by White's suggestion to make of the property a theater center as an adjunct to the Yale School of Drama.

Though the town approved his idea, the Yale Corporation did not. White took up the project on his own. He contacted O'Neill's widow, Carlotta, and obtained her permission to name the center after her notable husband – the only American playwright to win the Nobel Prize, recipient of four Pulitzer prizes, and a resident of nearby New London. By 1964, the project was under way with George C. White its president – a post he would hold until the year 2000.

The Theater Center is comprised of several buildings. The Theater Barn, pictured here, has a simple stage in an auditorium, rehearsal spaces, costume and dressing rooms. Rufus and Margo Rose of Waterford, for whom the Barn is named, were often billed as "America's foremost artists of the marionette theatre." They are best known for Margo's design and sculpting of the characters for the Howdy Doody Show from 1952 till 1960. Rufus operated Howdy.

The National Playwrights' Festival, a yearly event, reads about 800 plays from which it selects six to eight. The playwrights take up residence at the Center and receive direction to produce staged readings. The Festival, initiated in 1965, flourished under Lloyd Richards, Artistic Director from 1968 till 1999. Numerous well-known playwrights, including Wendy Wasserstein and August Wilson, have received impetus from their involvement with the O'Neill.

The O'Neill Center also hosts the National Puppetry Conference, the Cabaret & Performance Conference, the National Music Theater Conference, the National Critics Institute, and the Young Playwrights Festival. For information, go to www.oneilltheatercenter.org. or call: 860-443-5378

HARKNESS MEMORIAL STATE PARK

275 Great Neck Road, Waterford, Connecticut 06385

Eolia, the estate of Edward Harkness, was named for that Greek isle where Eolus, god of the winds, resided. Indeed there is a considerable fetch along Long Island Sound where Zephyr, the west wind, can attain a formidable presence; where Notus, the south wind, can waft gently across from Gardeners Bay. The lawns of *Eolia* run right down to the shore. The manor house itself, of forty-two rooms, stands on a little eminence with a broad, imposing view of the sea through ten points of the compass.

The father of Edward Harkness had the foresight to invest in Mr. Rockefeller's Standard Oil Company. In 1906, Edward purchased 230 acres of land and a manor house to adorn it. The most notable feature of the property is its gardens: Italian, Oriental and cutting gardens; greenhouses and shrubs. Extensive stonewalls enclose and adorn its many acres of plantings. A half-mile drive connects *Eolia* to Great Neck Road in Waterford.

Designed by Lord and Hewlett, *Eolia* combines 19th and 20th century Revival with Second Renaisance. Between 1918 and 1929, Beatrix Jones Farrand carried out extensive landscaping improvements.

In 1950, *Eolia* was willed to the State of Connecticut. In 1952, it became a state park. During the 1990's, Connecticut undertook restoration of the Harkness Estate. Roger and Peter Clarke, architects, and Rob Camp Fuoco, historic garden expert, joined to bring grandeur and beauty back to *Eolia*. The staff of the State Park Department, aided by the volunteers, Friends of Harkness, work continually to maintain and improve these notable gardens.

In 1986, the National Register of Historic Places added *Eolia*, more commonly known as *Harkness Memorial State Park*, to its registry, including the fifteen out buildings and a sturdy stone water tower. Though the park and gardens are open year round, the mansion itself can be visited only from Memorial Day to Labor Day. The house can be rented for functions by the day or by the hour. Be sure to visit *Eolia* when the flowers are blooming.

For information, go to www.stateparks.com/harkness_memorial.html or call 866–287–2757 toll free, 860–443–5725 locally.

HARBOR LIGHT
NEW LONDON
CONNECTICOT

1801

NEW LONDON HARBOR LIGHTHOUSE

Pequot Avenue, New London, Connecticut 06320

Latitude 41° 19' 00" N, Longitude 72° 05' 24'' W

Though John Winthrop, Jr., later governor of Connecticut, founded New London at the mouth of the Thames River in 1646, this port hadn't a beacon until 1750. By 1761, a stone tower 61' in height had been constructed on the site of the present lighthouse. The funding for it came from a public lottery.

Though the tower survived the attack by Benedict Arnold's British troops, who burned New London in 1781, it later developed a serious crack. In 1801, Abisha Woodward of New London built the present 89' octagonal brownstone tower, which is lined with brick. It cost over $15,000. New London Harbor Light is the oldest lighthouse in Connecticut; the seventh oldest in the nation. It was one of the earliest to have a flashing light to distinguish it from neighborhood lights.

By the mid 1800's, New London ranked only behind New Bedford and Nantucket as a whaling port. By 1852, a railroad depot existed beside the wharves, helping New London become a wealthy small center of commerce. The lighthouse keeper received a new house in 1818. In 1863 the present house was built; it was enlarged in 1900.

In 1857, the eleven lamps and their parabolic reflectors installed in 1834 were replaced by a fourth order Fresnel lens, still in service today. In 1912, the light was automated. The signal – a white light that stayed on three seconds, then off three seconds, having a red sector to show direction, recently became a fixed white light with a red sector. A fog signal was installed – a second-class Daboll trumpet – in 1874. A first-class signal usurped it 1883. A new siren in 1904 so upset the local people that a less obstreperous signal was installed. In 1911, the foghorn was moved to newly built Ledge Lighthouse [page 76].

In April 2005 the New London Maritime Society [page 90] became the new owners of the lighthouse through the National Historic Lighthouse Preservation Act of 2000. The National Register of Historic Places listed it in 1990. Though the lighthouse can be seen from Pequot Avenue, the tower and grounds are not open to the public. Please visit www.mlmaritimesociety.org or Jeremy D'Entremont's website, to which I am greatly indebted, at www.lighthouse.cc

Ledge Light
New London, Connecticut

LEDGE LIGHT

Mouth of the Thames River, New London, CT

Latitude 41° 18' 18" North, Longitude 72° 04' 42" West

A recent addition to Connecticut lighthouses, Ledge Light, formerly Southwest Ledge Light, began active duty 10 November 1909. In order to build a secure foundation on the ledge, builders Hamilton R. Douglas Company of New London, who also built the Groton Town Hall, constructed a massive wooden frame that they towed into position above the ledge. 82 feet square, it served as a form into which they poured rock and concrete. After fastening this to the ledge, they poured the 50-foot square foundation inside it. This foundation stands eighteen feet above low water. Accommodation was left for a basement.

The 3-storey lighthouse represents a combination of Colonial Revival and French Second Empire styles, popular with builders of this period. The cast iron light tower first held a fourth order Fresnel lens – now on view at the Customs House in New London [page 90].

Visible to 14 miles, the signal consists of three white flashes followed by a red in 30-second cycles. A foghorn was added in 1911 – two blasts every 20 seconds. The present light is a VRB-25 optic; focal plane 58'.

A ghost known as Ernie reputedly haunts Ledge Light. Supposedly a lighthouse keeper during the 1920's or 30's, whose wife ran off with the skipper of the Block Island ferry, leapt to his death from the roof, though it can't be verified. Stories of inexplicable doings still abound.

In 1939, Coast Guard crews took over as Ledge Light's keepers. In 1987, they automated the light. Today, the New London Ledge Light Foundation maintains and promotes the structure. The National Register of Historic Places listed Ledge Light in 1990. Ledge Light can be visited by boat tours run by Project Oceanology at the Avery Point, Groton, campus of the University of Connecticut. For information, call 860-445-9007 or 800-364-8472. Please visit www.oceanology.org and www.ledgelighthouse.org

For more information on Connecticut lighthouses, read *The Lighthouses of Connecticut* by Jeremy D'Entremont or visit his website, a trove of photos and information on New England lighthouses, www.lighthouse.cc, to which I am greatly indebted.

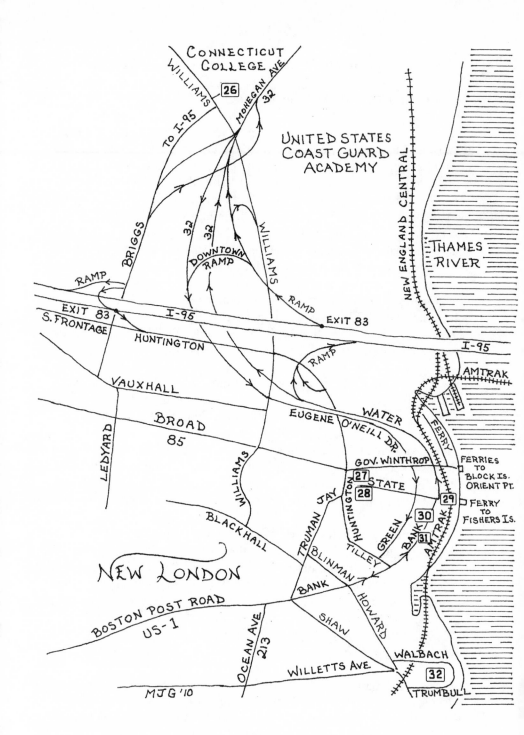

CONNECTICUT COLLEGE

26

UNITED STATES
COAST GUARD
ACADEMY

WILLIAMS

TO I-95

MOHEGAN AVE

32

32

32

DOWNTOWN RAMP

BRIGGS

WILLIAMS

RAMP

NEW ENGLAND CENTRAL

THAMES RIVER

RAMP

EXIT 83

S. FRONTAGE

I-95

EXIT 83

I-95

HUNTINGTON

AMTRAK

VAUXHALL

RAMP

LEDYARD

BROAD
85

WATER

EUGENE O'NEILL DR.

FERRY

WILLIAMS

GOV. WINTHROP

27

STATE

28

FERRIES
TO
BLOCK IS.
ORIENT PT.

29

FERRY
TO
FISHERS IS.

BLACKHALL

TRUMAN

JAY

HUNTINGTON

GREEN

BANK

30

AMTRAK

31

TILLEY

NEW LONDON

BLINMAN

BANK

HOWARD

SHAW

WALBACH

BOSTON POST ROAD
US-1

OCEAN AVE
213

WILLETTS AVE

32

MJG '10

TRUMBULL

NEW LONDON

#26	**LYMAN ALLYN ART MUSEUM**
#27	**GARDE THEATER**
#28	**NEW LONDON LIBRARY**
#29	**UNION RR STATION**
#30	**THE HYGIENIC**
#31	**US CUSTOMS HOUSE**
#32	**FORT TRUMBULL**

LYMAN ALLYN ART MUSEUM

625 Williams Street, New London, CT 06320

Lyman Allyn was born in Montville in 1797. He began as a sailor, and advanced to skipper of a whaling ship. In middle age he retired from the sea but managed a fleet of ships, and left a fortune to his children. The bulk of the estate eventually came to his daughter, Harriet.

Harriet, born in 1840, became widowed, without children, in 1893. She gave 40 acres of land along Williams Street in New London to found Connecticut College for Women. She supported the Lawrence Hospital and St. James Episcopal Church. Finally, she left a bequest upon her death in 1926 to construct an art museum in a landscaped park, and left an endowment to operate and maintain it. The building and park are reported to have cost $400,000 and stand between her home, the Deshon-Allyn House, and the campus of Connecticut College.

Her trustees selected Charles Adams Platt to be their architect. Known for his Freer Gallery in Washington, DC, Lyme Art Association [page 62], and Fanning Hall and Memorial Library at Connecticut College. Platt chose a neo-classical style built of local granite that approximated the buildings of the adjacent campus.

The museum had its grand opening on what would have been Harriet's 92nd birthday – 2 March 1932. Governor Wilbur Cross, Connecticut senators Frederic Walcott and Hiram Bingham, Dr. Katherine Blunt, president of Connecticut College, James May, Mayor of New London, and several museum directors, including Edward Waldo Forbes, curator of Harvard's Fogg Museum, attended the celebration.

Before it opened, The Lyman Allyn had received gifts, bequests, and loans. The trustees appointed Winslow Ames, a recent graduate of Harvard's Fogg School of Art, as the Lyman Allyn's first director. He proved a brilliant director and curator, and the Lyman Allyn flourished. In 1939, an addition was financed by a bequest from Virginia Palmer.

Claire Gaudiani, President of Connecticut College, brought the Lyman Allyn under its aegis in 1996. The present director, Dr. Nancy Stula, maintains over 15,000 works of fine art. For more information, go to www.lymanallyn.org or call 860-443-2545. For a definitive history of the LAAM, read Jackwyn Thompson Durrschmidt's book, "the finest small museum in the country," to which I am greatly indebted.

GARDE THEATRE

325 State Street, New London, Connecticut 06320

The Garde stands on the site of the former mansion of William Williams, a whaling merchant. The Garde site was purchased from the Williams estate by Theodore Bodenwein, founder of the New London Day. He sold the property to developer Arthur Friend, builder of movie houses. The architect of the theater, named for local businessman Walter Garde, was Arland Johnson.

The Garde opened 22 September 1926 and became a success at presenting Vaudeville and film. One of the great movie palaces of its time, its sumptuous Moroccan interior, designed and painted by Vera Leeper of Denver, depicts North African desert, mountains, caravans, and Moorish market scenes. The extensive stencil work simulates Bedouin carpet patterns.

1472 seats, a huge video screen, and excellent acoustics attracted Warner Brothers, who purchased the Garde in 1929 for a million dollars. It continued to be the area's premier movie house until the advent of multiplex cinemas. Warner Brothers sold the Garde in 1978. It hobbled along until 1985, when the Garde Arts Center, a new non-profit corporation, purchased it for $300,000. Under the direction of Steve Sigel, the Garde produced dance, musical theater, and contemporary music. In 1987, the Eastern Connecticut Symphony Orchestra took up residence. In 1994, movies were again added to the bill.

In 1994, a $15.75 million fundraiser began, to restore and renew the Garde. Elevators and wheelchair access were added. The Oasis Room, with 3500 square feet, now serves as a function hall and catering kitchen. The architectural firm of Hannivan & Company, of Toronto, took over the restoration of the lobbies and auditorium. Local artist Elaine Mills and local sculptress Jennifer Collins aided in the restoration. New lobbies, offices, concessions and restrooms have brought this grand facility up to date.

New acoustics, stage equipment, and lighting have made the Garde an excellent venue for any sort of music or entertainment. The Garde's interior is a work of art not to be missed. For information go to www.gardearts.org or email info@gardearts.org For tickets call 860–444- 7373.

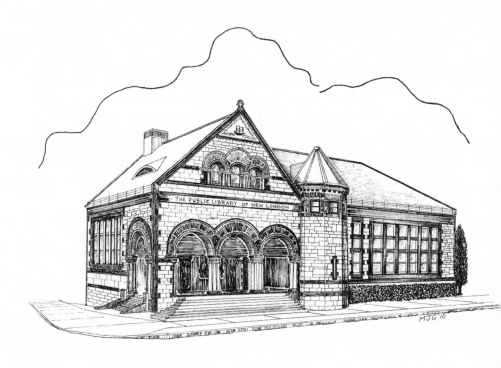

THE PUBLIC LIBRARY OF NEW LONDON

MJG 10

PUBLIC LIBRARY OF NEW LONDON

63 Huntington Street, New London, Connecticut 06320

Henry P. Havens, a wealthy whaling, sealing, and shipping magnate, died in 1867. He left a third of his estate to his daughter, a third to his son, and a third to be used for the city of New London. When his son died, the trustees chose to use this wealth to construct a public library. In 1890, his daughter, Mrs. Anna H. Perkins, died and left her share of the estate to the public library.

Henry Hobson Richardson was a famous architect of the 19th century. His other contribution to New London was the Union Railroad Station [page 86]. His death in 1887 precluded his seeing the completion of his library, but his son-in-law, George Foster Shepley, of Shepley, Rutan, and Coolidge, carried on. The firm sent young George Warren Cole to supervise the project. Cole went on to design several buildings in New London as well as the Deep River Town Hall [page 22].

Construction began in May 1889. $50,000, an enormous sum in those days, was spent on the new library, completed in July 1891. Richardson's design was Romanesque – the groined arches of the entryway are not only attractive but also extremely strong. The turret and the gables with their elaborate Romanesque arches of Kibbe sandstone trim set off the pinkish granite from Worcester, Massachusetts.

The original building is parallelogram in shape – forty by ninety feet. At the peak of the porch roof the coat of arms of New London is displayed – a ship under full sail. A panel by the entrance depicts Henry P. Havens in bronze relief, executed by famous sculptor, Augustus St. Gaudens. The main room, now the children's room, features a sculpted brownstone fireplace, and oak panels from floor to thirteen-foot ceilings. The ceiling is of oak sheathing between exposed beams. The rooms are naturally well lighted and inviting. The National Register of Historic Places added the library to its list in 1970.

In the 1970's, Rick Gipstein of Lindsay, Liebig, and Roche Architects of 320 State Street, designed an addition. Today, the Public Library of New London is known for its collection of books on whaling and local genealogy. The library was originally home to the New London County Historical Society from its founding in 1870 until 1907.

For more information go to www.plnl.org or call 860–447–1411.

UNION STATION

27 Water Street, New London, Connecticut 06320

Union Station proved the last project of the famed architect, Henry Hobson Richardson [1838–1887]. Commissioned in 1885, it replaced the earlier depot of 1852. Since its opening in 1889 it has been the centerpiece and the pride of downtown New London. Built for the New York, New Haven & Hartford RR and the Vermont Central, it served the Northeast Corridor – the Boston to Washington, DC route – and brought further prosperity to this small but thriving port city.

It now serves the Acela Express, Northeast Regional, and Shore Line East railroads. It connects travelers to Greyhound Bus that shares the station, and Southeast Area Transit. As the station backs up to the Thames River, it also connects to the Cross Sound Ferry to Orient Point, NY. 159,000 passengers used Union Station in 2009.

In 1976, the consortium that had recently purchased the building began restoration, directed by the architect, George Notter. From the wooden wainscoting and burnt sienna plaster walls to the heavily beamed ceiling and decorative exterior brickwork, Union Station now appears much as it did a century ago. Since 1971, Union Station has been in the National Register of Historic Places. It also provides the logogram of www.newlondonlandmarks.org

SOLDIERS' & SAILORS' MONUMENT

46 State Street, New London, Connecticut

Joseph Lawrence, born Giuseppe Lorenzo in Venice, Italy, in 1788, came to America and made a fortune whaling out of New London. His sons carried on his estate and gave generously to their hometown. They endowed the Lawrence Hospital and donated memorials to local members of the armed services and fire department who had lost their lives to save others.

This 50' obelisk was designed and fabricated by Smith Granite Company of nearby Westerly, RI, and dedicated on 6 May 1896. The figures on the pedestal represent a soldier and a sailor. The nine foot high female figure surmounting the monument represents Peace, and cradles a palm frond in her arms.

THE HYGIENIC

83 Bank Street, New London, Connecticut 06320

In 1781, Benedict Arnold and his British troops captured Fort Trumbull in New London [page 92], and burned the city of New London to the ground. The foundations of old colonials on Bank Street were filled in. In 1844, Captain Harris, a prosperous whaler, built a Greek Revival building at 83 Bank Street to serve as ship's store and quarters for his crews. By 1878, the building was known as the Columbia Hotel. The storefront of brick arches was replaced with columns; slate shingles replaced cedar shingles on the roof; and four dormers were added.

In 1919, a restaurant run by the Swanson Brothers opened. In 1931, the Sigros family purchased the business and named it the Hygienic, Hygia being the Greek goddess of health. The Hygienic Restaurant became an all night restaurant with rooms to let upstairs. During the 1940's and 1950's the Hygienic remained respectable. Franklin Rooseveldt lunched here in between trains. Rumor has it that Al Capone did likewise.

It later devolved into a hangout of ill repute. Bank Street, by the 1960's and 70's, was known for its less than salutary delights. In 1979, local artists convinced the owner to have an art show there. The show would be non-juried, non-censored, without an exhibit or admission fee. But The Hygienic closed in 1985 and stood vacant for ten years. In 1996 it was scheduled for demolition. Local artists made an effort to save it and, in 1998, purchased the building.

Hygienic Art, Inc. has greatly aided in the renewal of New London's downtown economy and reputation. The Hygienic, no longer a restaurant, hosts artists, poets, playwrights and musicians. In 2000, the building was restored, with additional performance and gallery space in its basement. In 2001, the adjacent lot began its transformation into an al fresco performance space and sculpture garden. With support from the city, local businesses, and private patrons, the Hygienic has been renewed as a memorable art space. Each January, the *Salon des Independants* holds its non-juried, non-censored exhibition. During the same week, poetry, theater, music and dance take place in the neighborhood. In 2010, we celebrated Hygienic XXXI.

Hygienic Arts Inc. has an extensive website filled with art, events, history, directions, artwork submission forms and film clips. Go to www.hygienic.org or call 860 – 443 – 8001.

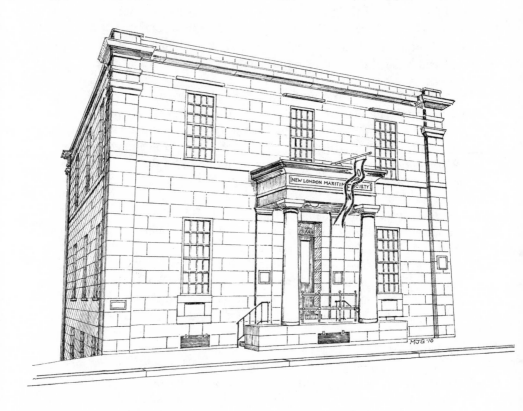

U. S. CUSTOM HOUSE - 1833

150 Bank Street, New London, Connecticut 06320

Robert Mills [1781–1855] became the nation's first federal architect. A student of Benjamin H. LaTrobe, designer of our nation's capitol, Mills designed numerous public buildings in Washington, DC. His Ionic Treasury Building, Doric Patent Office [now the National Portrait Gallery], Corinthian Federal Post Office, and towering Washington Monument still stand today. Between 1833 and 1835, he designed four customhouses: New London, CT; Newburyport, MA; New Bedford, MA; and Middletown, CT. All but the last still exist. Mills also left us two books: *The American Pharos, or Lighthouse Guide*, and *A Guide to the Capitol of the United States*.

His customhouses reflected the current penchant for the Greek Revival style. Simple, austere, and nearly unadorned, they present a front of elegance and respectability. He incorporated in all four the newly conceived idea of building a fireproof building: each has walls and roof of solid masonry. Masonry vaulted arches rather than wooden beams support the floors. Much of the vaulting in this Custom House is of brick. The paired front doors are of massive oak – wrought of planks from the USS Constitution.

By the 1840's, New London burgeoned as an important commercial port. Ships from foreign ports had to declare their cargoes and pay duties, or customs. In 1839, the mutinous Mendi Africans from *La Amistad* were brought to this Custom House. In 1858, a fugitive, stowaway slave was tried here. The Connecticut Personal Liberty Act took precedence over the Fugitive Slave Act, and the man went free.

By 1983, the federal government declared this Custom House superfluous. The New London Maritime Society restored the building and converted it to a museum, but the top floor remains an active custom office - the oldest customhouse in America in continuous service. The National Register of Historic Places listed it in 1970.

The Custom House Maritime Museum features the Jibboom Club, or society of whalers, an artifacts collection, ship models, artwork, the Frank L. McGuire Maritime Research Library, the Archibald J. Chester, Jr. Reading Room, and a gift shop. The Maritime Society sponsors lectures, exhibits, and parades all year round. Visit them at www.nlmaritimesociety.org or call 860-447-2501.

Fort Trumbull 1777 rebuilt 1852
Fort Neck on the Thames River
New London, Connecticut

MJG '89

FORT TRUMBULL

90 Walbach Street, New London, Connecticut 06320

Governor John Trumbull, for whom this fort is named, ordered it built in 1775, at the beginning of the American Revolution, to protect New London Harbor. Notwithstanding, Benedict Arnold, commanding 2500 British troops, captured the fort in 1781. Arnold went on to burn shipping on the Thames, attack New London and burn it to the ground.

Between 1839 and 1852, Fort Trumbull was redesigned and rebuilt as it presently stands. An irregular pentagram in shape, its three shorter sides face the river. Of the 42 forts built during this era for coastal defense, collectively known as the Third System of Fortifications, Fort Trumbull stands unique. Its architecture follows the style of Egyptian Revival. Army engineer George Washington Cullum supervised the construction.

During the Civil War, Fort Trumbull served to organize Union troops and as headquarters for the U. S. 14th Infantry Regiment. At the beginning of the 20th century several modern Endicott era forts were built to guard Long Island Sound. Fort Trumbull served as their headquarters. In 1910, the Revenue Cutter Service – later renamed the Coast Guard – was given Fort Trumbull to use as an academy until they moved to their present campus in 1932.

From 1939-1946, Ft. Trumbull trained Merchant Marine officers to serve in World War II. From 1946-1950, it served as part of the University of Connecticut, to educate veterans under the GI Bill. From 1950-1970, it was part of Naval Underwater Sound Laboratory, which developed sonar systems for submarines. From 1970-1996, it continued as part of Naval Underwater Systems Center, later the Naval Undersea Warfare Center.

After extensive restoration, Fort Trumbull State Park opened in 2000. The National Register of Historic Places listed it in 1972. The park is open year round. The Fort, Visitor Center and gift shop open from Memorial Day till Columbus Day. The inside of Fort Trumbull has been restored to its 19th century standards. The Visitors Center boasts computerized interactive exhibits, multi media theaters, 3-D models, graphics and literature.

For more information call: 860–444– 591 or visit www.fortfriends.org

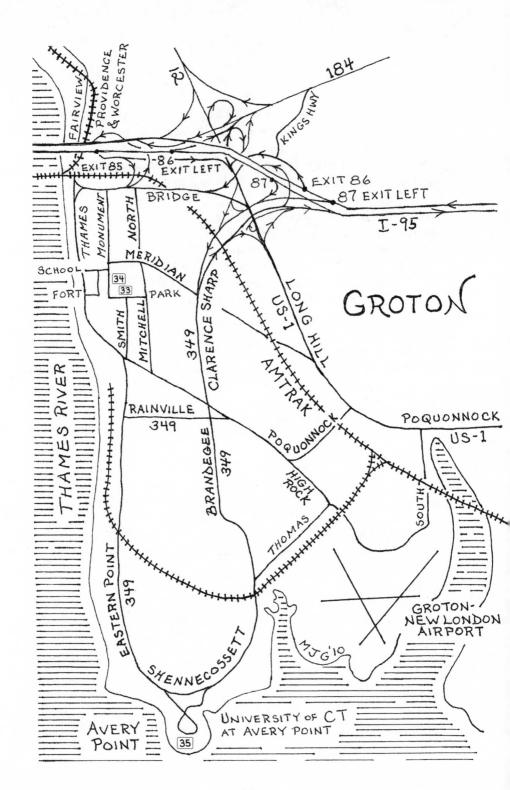

GROTON

FORT GRISWOLD

57 Fort Street, Groton, Connecticut 06340

A native of Norwich, CT, General Benedict Arnold was familiar with nearby New London and Groton. He carried out a ruthless campaign against these towns. After defeating the militia at Fort Trumbull, New London [page 92], he followed the refugees across the Thames River to Groton. The Battle of Groton Heights was fought on 6 September 1781.

Knowing the layout of Fort Griswold, Arnold landed his troops where its cannon couldn't be aimed. The Colonial militia numbered about 150; the British about 800. Called on to surrender, Colonel William Ledyard flatly refused. Colonel Eyre, the British commander, warned him to expect no quarter. After 40 minutes of fierce fighting, the British overran the fort. Colonel Ledyard and several dozen Patriots were slain – reportedly after Colonel Ledyard surrendered his sword.

The British claimed 51 dead and 142 wounded; the Militia 88 dead, 35 wounded, and 28 taken prisoner. The seriously wounded militiamen took refuge in the house of Ebenezer Avery on Thames Street. This proved the largest battle of the Revolution to take place in Connecticut. It is celebrated every year at Fort Griswold.

Though Fort Griswold was rebuilt, no further battle was ever fought at this site, though the British blockaded the river in 1814. In 1830, the Town of Groton raised a commemorative obelisk of local granite. A plaque on the gatepost outside the fortress bears the names of the dead. In 1881, the battle's centennial, the obelisk received a peaked roof that raised its height to 135 feet. The oldest war memorial of this type, the Monument rises above the trees on Fort Hill – visible for miles.

The State now owns Fort Griswold Battlefield State Park. The National Register of Historic Places listed it in 1970. The stone caretaker's house nearby dates from 1830. The Daughters of the American Revolution have held their meetings there for over a century, and now run it as a gift shop and museum. The Avery House was moved to the site in 1971. The fort and all three buildings are open, free of charge, from Memorial Day to Labor Day. Climbing the 166 steps of the obelisk results in spectacular views. The cannon pictured came from the Spanish flagship, Marie-Theresa, captured in Cuba during the Spanish American War. For information go to www.fortgriswold.org or call: 860-445-1729.

BILL MEMORIAL LIBRARY 1890

BILL MEMORIAL LIBRARY

240 Monument Street, Groton, Connecticut 06340

Frederick Bill, 1833-1920, grew up in that part of Groton that now is Ledyard. He taught school, sold books, and worked with his brother publishing books in Springfield, Massachusetts. Following the Civil War, he invested in the importation and manufacture of linen goods and grew wealthy enough to retire at the age of forty. He bought 63 acres along the Thames River in Groton, where he built a wooden mansion at 443 Eastern Point Road. His widow bequeathed the land to Connecticut College in 1935. The property eventually passed to the Ameralda Hess Oil Company, which tore down the mansion.

In 1888, Frederick Bill purchased 1700 books to start a library in memory of his sisters, Eliza and Harriet. Architect Stephen C. Earle designed this library, built of granite from Stony Creek, Connecticut, trimmed with Maynard freestone, and having a red slate roof. The dedication of the library took place 18 June 1890.

In 1907, Mr. Bill had an addition built to match the existing structure. He planned to enlarge the reading room and include a small museum. The Bill today still displays that collection of butterflies and paintings. In 1994, another addition was made to house a reference room and offices.

Bill also supported the Groton Congregational Church, paid for the Groton Heights School, and endowed Connecticut College in New London, who named a hall for him.

Today the Bill Library houses over 21,000 items. It is a member of the Connecticut Library Consortium and participates in iConn – Connecticut's database. Computers and WiFi are available. The Friends of the Bill are active and loyal, and host book sales, book discussions, lectures, meditation groups, and story times for small children.

The Bill Memorial Library stands high on Groton Heights adjacent to Fort Griswold Battlefield State Park [page 96]. The view of the Thames River Valley from this gem of a library is remarkable.

For information go to www.billmemorial.org or call 860-445-0392.

BRANFORD HOUSE - 1904

1084 Shennecossett Road, Groton, Connecticut 06340

In 1899, wealthy steamship and railroad magnate Henry Bradley Plant passed away and left a fortune of $22,000,000. His only son, Morton, 47, received two thirds of this. Ever lavish, Morton Plant also knew how to invest. At the time of his own death in 1918, his estate amounted to $50,000,000. Plant gave $1,000,000 to Connecticut College. He gave the present brick town hall to Groton, repaired roads, subsidized a baseball team, and established a trolley line.

More interested in being a gentleman farmer than joining the social set in Newport, Rhode Island, Plant built his summer mansion in Groton. His wife, Nellie, who had studied architecture at the Sorbonne, collaborated with English architect Robert W. Gibson to design Branford House – named for the town where Morton Plant was born. Basically Tudor in style, Branford House boasts 31 rooms. Its interior has a plenitude of styles – Baroque, Gothic, Classical, and Renaissance. The interior panels of oak, walnut, and mahogany are exquisite. The culmination of this woodwork is the two story high surround of the large fireplace in the front room. Marble, onyx, and sandstone are carved to make pillars, fireplaces, and panels. The winding staircase was built of Italian marble. The extensive gardens were filled with granite and marble carvings, pools and fountains. The cost of this mansion was $3,000,000.

Plant purchased two local farms, nearby Pine Island, and the shabby Fort Griswold House near Avery Point. He replaced it with the stylish Griswold Hotel – an immense, upscale resort for the wealthy set. His farms raised food for his hotel, family and permanent staff of 50. Plant used Branford House but a month or two per year. When he died in 1918, it passed to his son, Henry, then to his daughter-in-law. It was auctioned in 1939 for $55,000 to the State of CT, who deeded it to the U. S. Coastguard in 1941 as a training center. It was stipulated they build a lighthouse at Avery Point to commemorate Coastguardsmen and lighthouse keepers. The lighthouse stayed active till 1967, at which time the Coast Guard relocated. Branford House became part of the Avery Point Campus of the University of CT. The Alexey von Schlippe Gallery of Art on the second floor of the mansion should not be missed. The National Register of Historic Places listed Branford House in 1984. It can be leased by the day for private or business functions. For information visit www.branford.uconn.edu or call 860-405-9072

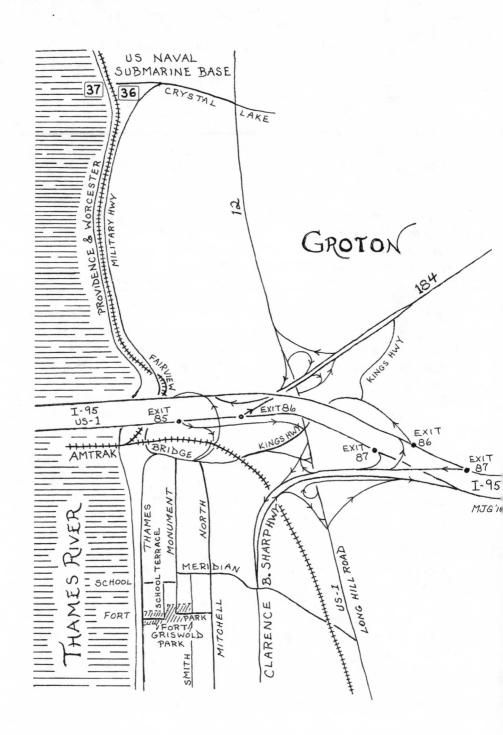

US NAVAL
SUBMARINE BASE

CRYSTAL LAKE

37 36

PROVIDENCE & WORCESTER

MILITARY HWY

12

GROTON

184

FAIRVIEW

KINGS HWY

I-95
US-1

EXIT 85

EXIT 86

KINGS HWY

EXIT 86

AMTRAK

BRIDGE

EXIT 87

EXIT 87

I-95

MJG'10

THAMES RIVER

THAMES TERRACE

MONUMENT

NORTH

SCHOOL TERRACE

MERIDIAN

CLARENCE B. SHARP HWY

US-1

LONG HILL ROAD

SCHOOL

FORT

PARK
/FORT/
GRISWOLD
PARK

SMITH

MITCHELL

102

GROTON

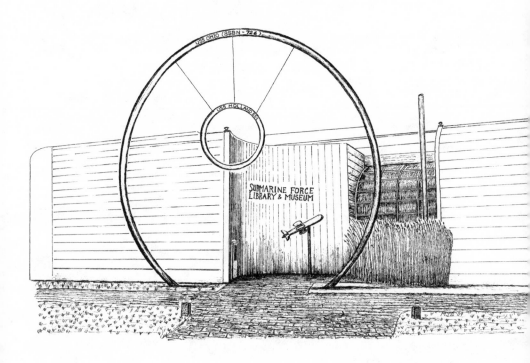

SUBMARINE FORCE LIBRARY & MUSEUM

One Crystal Lake Road, Groton, Connecticut 06340

Located on the east bank of the Thames River in Groton, just outside the gates of the Submarine Base, the Submarine Force Library and Museum not only boasts films and books and artifacts within, but also has the world's first nuclear powered submarine, USS Nautilus SSN 571 [page 106], docked alongside in the river.

Electric Boat – that division of General Dynamics Corporation that builds submarines in Groton, just downriver, established the submarine library, then donated their entire collection to the Navy in 1964. They housed it at the New London [actually Groton] Submarine Base. In 1969, the name, *Submarine Force Library and Museum* was adopted.

This is the only submarine museum operated by the U. S. Navy. Consequently, it contains over 33,000 artifacts, 20,000 documents, and 30,000 photographs, as well as a library of over 6,000 volumes that includes an 1870 copy of Jules Verne's famous novel *20,000 Leagues Under the Sea*. The library and museum are open to anyone who desires to research submarines or their history.

In addition to the Nautilus, the museum also boasts a couple of midget submarines of World War II vintage, and a replica of David Bushnell's *Turtle*. Bushnell designed and built his one-man vessel in 1775. True to its name, Turtle resembles two turtle shells stuck together. She had a rudder; both a vertical and horizontal propeller driven by hand cranks; a ballast tank and pump for submerging or surfacing; and windows in her conning tower for surveillance. The goal to attach a bomb to the bottom of the British ship of war, *Eagle*, never reached fruition. The present replica, built by Joe Leary and Fred Frise, is on loan from the Connecticut River Museum in Essex [page 28].

The submarine Nautilus [page 106] is open for inspection. A 30-minute self-guided audio tour of the vessel is provided.

The museum is very child friendly, but also geared to the serious researcher. A gift shop on the premises deals in books and cards and memorabilia. The library and museum are open year round. Admission and parking are free. For information go to www.submarinemuseum.com or call 800-343-0079 or 860-694-3174.

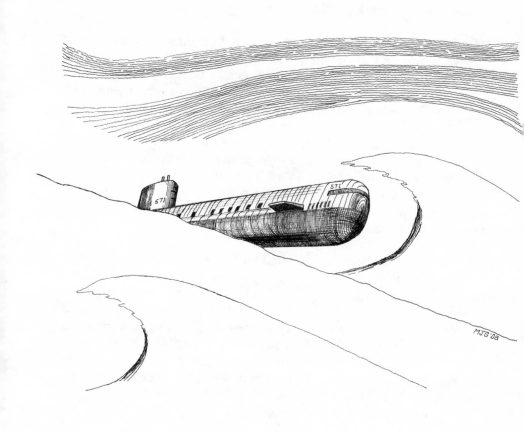

USS NAUTILUS SSN 571

Now docked at the Submarine Force Museum
One Crystal Lake Road, Groton, Connecticut 06340

On 21 January 1954, I enjoyed the privilege of watching First Lady Mamie Eisenhower break a bottle of Champagne over the prow of the Nautilus before she slid down the ways. Years of research and hard work had produced the world's first nuclear powered submarine.

At the Naval Reactors Branch of the Atomic Energy Commission, under the directorship of Captain [later Admiral] Hyman Rickover, a group of engineers and scientists developed a power plant suitable for submarines. In 1974, the Energy Research and Development Administration and the Nuclear Regulatory Commission took over the functions of the Atomic Energy Commission.

By July 1951, Congress authorized the building of the Nautilus. The name derives from the Greek word *nautilos* – sailor. She would be the fourth U. S. Naval vessel with that name. President Harry S. Truman laid her keel 14 June 1952 at the Electric Boat Division of General Dynamics Corp in Groton, Connecticut. They launched her on 21 January 1954. The Navy commissioned her on 30 September 1954.

On 17 January 1955, nearly a year after her historic splash into the Thames River, the newest Nautilus steamed off. She set new speed and distance records over the next few years. In 1958, with her crew of 116, the Nautilus departed Pearl Harbor, Hawaii, and steamed beneath the ice cap of the Arctic and out the other side. On 3 August, she logged her arrival at the North Pole.

In 1960 she joined the Sixth Fleet in the Mediterranean. After years of service and developmental testing, she was decommissioned on 3 March 1980, having logged over 500,000 miles during 25 years. In 1979, the National Register of Historic Places listed the Nautilus. In 1982, the Secretary of the Interior listed her as a National Historic Landmark.

On 11 April 1986, exactly 86 years from the inception of the Submarine Force, The Nautilus joined The Submarine Force Museum [page 104] as a permanent exhibit at the museum's grand opening. The Nautilus is now open to the public. For information visit www.submarinemuseum.com or call: 800-343-0079 or 860-694-3174.

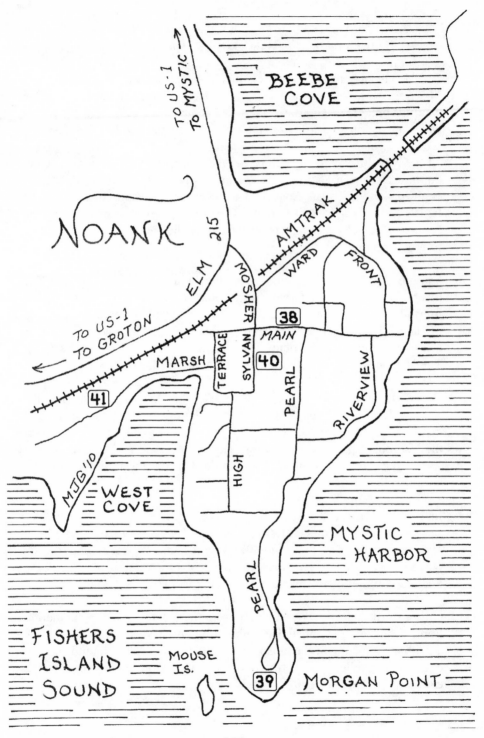

NOANK

BEEBE COVE

TO US-1 TO MYSTIC

AMTRAK

ELM 215

TO US-1 TO GROTON

WARD

FRONT

MOSHER

SYLVAN

38

MAIN

40

TERRACE

MARSH

PEARL

RIVERVIEW

41

MJG'10

HIGH

WEST COVE

MYSTIC HARBOR

PEARL

FISHERS ISLAND SOUND

MOUSE Is.

39

MORGAN POINT

NOANK

CANDY SODA
PERIODICALS
NOVELTIES
SMOKES

CARSONS STORE
ESTABLISHED 1907

ICE CREAM
SUNDRIES
COFFEE
CONVERSATION

BREAKFAST/LUNCH · ICE CREAM CONES · ICE COLD ICE

MJG '08

CARSON'S VARIETY STORE - 1907

43 Main Street, Noank, Connecticut 06340

I step into Carson's, perch atop one of the green, revolving stools at the counter, and start with coffee. I never know what may proceed from that point onward. It may be to discuss art with the waitress, or the weather with the old man who comes in every morning for his paper. It sometimes leads to milkshakes, homemade donuts and euphoria.

During the off-season, it's mostly regulars in here: older folks having tea with their English muffin; children, fresh from their classes, asking for ice cream. In a month or two, business will start to perk up. Noank has summer residents, five marinas, and two yacht clubs. Boats in Noank far outnumber the people. This is as it should be. Most of the boats I've known were comely, well mannered, and fair-spoken. And not one of them has ever tracked snow into Carson's.

Carson's can seat about two dozen people – as long as a few of them sit outside on the porch. Dogs are welcome, except for those who criticize the donuts. I'm guilty of keeping a sailboat at Noank, and working on boats to support my writing habit. More than a couple of times, I've spent a rainy hour in Carson's, drinking coffee and writing in my journal.

In 1907, Jane Carson opened a store and lunchroom at the west end of Main Street, near the tracks. When that building burned, she moved to another at the east end of Main by the Mystic River. In 1918, she purchased a house and had an out building moved by mule team to the present location to become her store. Her son, Bernie, took over management of the store in 1935 and ran it till 1973. Present owner David Blacker ensures that the atmosphere of neighborliness presides. Carson's is a part of the Noank Historic District.

It seems to me that a village as pretty as Noank deserves an institution. Carson's is a place to relax and eat Loretta's homemade black bean soup or excellent omelets. It's a place to share your newspaper with the stranger sitting beside you. It's a place to remind us that Noank remains the most peaceful little peninsula in Connecticut.

For information call 860-536-0059, or, better still, stop in.

MORGAN POINT LIGHTHOUSE

Pearl Street, Noank, Connecticut 06340

41° 19.00' N, 71° 59.37' W

In 1831, the federal government decided to put a lighthouse at Morgan Point to aid mariners trying to get into West Cove, Noank, to the west, or into Mystic Harbor to the east. On land purchased from shipbuilder Roswell Avery Morgan, a twenty-five foot granite tower was erected on the point. A granite light keeper's house was built beside it.

The original ten oil lamps with reflectors were found to be too dim, and in 1855, they replaced them with a 6th-order Fresnel lens. As shipbuilding and commerce in Mystic Harbor increased, the need for a better light became evident. In 1868, a two-story granite building of eight rooms with a slate roof and octagonal iron light tower was constructed. The height of the tower is 52 feet; the focal plane 61 feet.

This same design – "Victorian Gothic Revival" - was incorporated into five other lighthouses in southern New England. Henry Davis, later appointed U. S. Assistant Superintendent of Lifesaving Stations, supervised the building of the Morgan Point Light.

The first keeper of the new light was Alexander McDonald. When he died in 1869, his wife Francis kept the light for two years. She then turned over her duties to her brother, Thaddeus Pecor of Mystic, who kept the light for 48 years. During a fierce winter, he helped save the lives of survivors of a wreck off Seaflower Reef. He finally retired in 1919. It is said that the ghost of Thaddeus still haunts Morgan Point Light, but his great granddaughter, Hazel Matey of Ledyard, assures me that the old man would never harm anyone.

The last keeper, a man named Reilly, had but a two-year tenure. In 1921, an automated light on a steel tower was built at the mouth of Mystic Harbor on Crooks Ledge. The decommissioned lighthouse has been privately owned ever since and is not open to the public.

In 1978, The National Register of Historic Places included Morgan Point Light as part of the Noank Historic District. More information can be found at the Sylvan Street Museum [page 114] or in Jeremy D'Entremont's book, *The Lighthouses of Connecticut.* Please visit his fine website, to which I am greatly indebted, at www.lighthouse.cc.

THE SYLVAN STREET MUSEUM

17 Sylvan Street, Noank, Connecticut 06340

In 1899, the Reverend Herbert L. Mitchell resigned from his Episcopal parish in Yantic, CT, and came to Mystic and Noank as a missionary. In 1900, the Episcopalians of Noank established their church. They first held services and Sunday school in the Golden Cross Lodge at the foot of Main Street. In 1901, Mr. and Mrs. Edward Grumley of Noank sold the Church a parcel of land on Sylvan Street. Mrs. William Johnson is remembered for her unflagging energy in raising funds through rummage sales and chicken potpie suppers at the old Town Hall.

Reverend Mitchell and some of his parish collected fieldstone for building. The mason, Charles Shirley, brought most of the stone from Fishers Island. By 1902, the 20' by 30' building had been completed and consecrated. First known as the Church of the Ascension, it came to be known as Grace Church. Some believe this change memorialized Grace Johnson, who died in 1896. Her mother, Mrs. William Johnson, gave the church a stained glass window in her memory.

The first minister, Reverend Albert C. Jones, also served Saint Marks Parish of Mystic. The church remained fulltime until 1936. Until 1960, it served as a summer chapel. From 1960 till 1963, it resumed year round status, but reverted in 1963 to a summer chapel. In 1966, Grace Church was deconsecrated and given to the Noank Fire District. In 1967, the Fire District gave Grace Church to the Historical Society.

Dozens of volunteers undertook a massive cleanup and restoration. Local people donated artifacts, maps and pictures; Mystic Seaport donated half models and pictures. The museum held its grand opening on July 4th, 1967. Since then, they have been a repository for artifacts and archives, helping people in genealogical research and enlightening the community about the impressive maritime heritage of this village.

Noank Historical Society now uses the former Latham Chester Store at 108 Main Street in Noank as a lecture and exhibition hall. In 1979, the National Register of Historic Places designated all of Noank east of Elm Street, including the museum and store, an historic district. The Historical Society also sponsors an art exhibit from Independence Day through Labor Day. Their quarterly, *Noank Ledger,* contains information on current or forthcoming events. For more information visit www.noankhistoricalsociety.org or call 860-536-3021.

NOANK FOUNDRY

70 Marsh Road, Noank, Connecticut 06340

In 1908, a substation and repair shop was built at 70 Marsh Road in Noank to service trolleys of the Groton and Stonington Street Railway. Their trolleys served the shoreline from 1904 till 1928. Most of the trolley tracks were torn up but, yesterday, I saw a yard of glinting rail where the pavement had been dug up in downtown Mystic.

During the late 1930's, an artist used the Noank shop to paint murals for the 1939-1940 World's Fair in New York City. In the late 1940's, the trolley shop became a foundry that specialized in iron castings: fire backs, boat parts and machine components. I can remember my father taking me here as a little boy back in the 50's. Inside, it seemed dark and dirty, hot and smoky. Sand boxes and patterns and iron ingots and piles of unfinished castings filled the foundry; sand and slag littered the floor.

All that has changed. By the 1990's, the foundry went out of business. In 2003, a blacksmith took over the shop. A forge replaced the furnaces. Wrought iron gates and grills emerged from the smithy. But the blacksmith was not content solely with function. He incorporated beauty into his gates. He twisted and hammered his metals into sculpture. His work has become fine art. One of his latest creations, a raven in flight, is a thing of grandeur.

A few years later, he invited several sculptors to share his space. They now offer classes in drawing, sculpture, and molding. Soon, the space became a studio and a showroom for a variety of artisans.

Now known as the Noank Foundry, Sculpture Studio & Garden Gate Blacksmith, this old brick building bustles with a dynamic, creative energy. The Noank Foundry Artists host a show put on by their members.

The Noank Foundry is open year round. For more information visit www.facebook.com/pages/Noank-Foundry-Artist-studios/131890694553

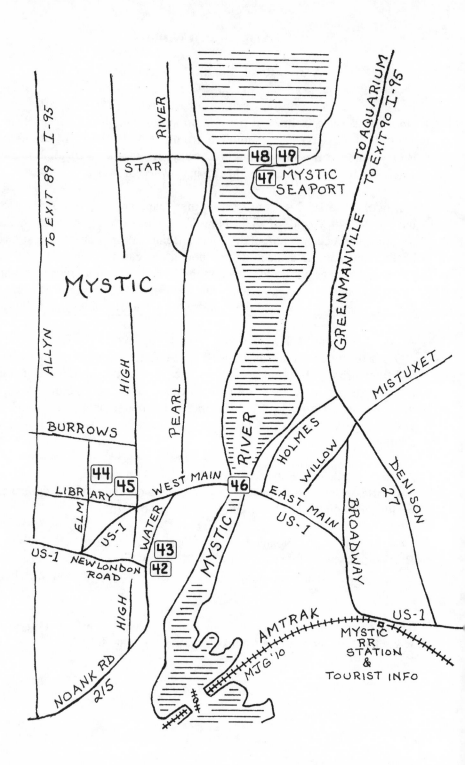

MYSTIC

THE EMPORIUM

15 Water Street, Mystic, Connecticut 06355

In 1859, two owners of shares in local whalers, Isaac Randall and Dwight Ashby, built a two and a half storey retail shop at 15 Water Street. Over the next century, the building often changed owners and saw duty as various stores and as a boarding house. During the 1930's, it housed a grocery store as well as apartments. By 1965 it was so neglected that it sold for $3000.

Later that year, actor Leland Howard and artist Paul White purchased the building to use as an art space, gallery and store. They named their shop The Emporium. They stocked it with Victoriana: antique toys, recorded calliope music, paper flowers, old posters and beeswax candles. Rather than an artist's studio, space was found for a French gourmet shop, with imported delicacies and enameled cookware.

In 1978 the two sold their shop to Robert Bankel and Evan Nickles. They hired manager Cindy Cobb, who has given herself to The Emporium, heart and soul. And she doesn't mind that the ghosts of two small boys from the 1800's, Billy and Willy, haunt the building.

The Emporium has acquired an eclectic collection of antiques, toys, novelties, jewelry, toiletries, and clothing. You can purchase a silver bangle, a silk scarf, or a genuine 1938 Seeburg jukebox. If you need a card for any occasion, choose from their huge selection. Downstairs you'll find toys, coloring books, Halloween masks, and seashells.

In the 2nd floor gallery local artists display work in mediums as various as fabric, photography, watercolors and sculpture. The Emporium has ambiance; the floorboards are wide, the thresholds worn; the front door thumb latch needs to be spoken to gently; the elderly glass display cases are often for sale. The cash register dates from 1921. The Emporium is a part of the Mystic River Historic District.

The outside of the building is painted olive. It's trimmed in a green just the verdant side of teal with buttercup colored panels; its many sashes are painted vermillion. It has three front doors with broad granite steps from a time when various businesses shared the building. It's funky, it's quaint, it's been a destination in downtown Mystic for forty years. Call them at 860-536-3891.

MYSTIC ARTS CENTER

9 Water Street, Mystic, CT 06355

In 1892 artist Charles Davis visited Mystic. He was taken with the lovely landscapes reminiscent of the Barbizon region of France. In 1913, he and Dr. George Leonard formed the Society of Mystic Artists and held their first show at the Broadway School. In 1930, they incorporated as the Mystic Art Association.

By then, a number of prominent artists had found their ways to Mystic. They began to attract the attention of critics and reviewers in Boston, New York, and Hartford. By 1928, The Art Association planned a permanent gallery and the artists subscribed to a bond to finance the building. The gallery opened 23 July 1931. 1946 saw the first of the many themed Artists Balls that took place annually till 1959.

By 1947, the Association held two shows every summer. By 1955, they invited artists outside the Mystic area to participate. In 1959, they held the first Mystic Outdoor Art Festival. In 1960, the two-man show of John Gregoropoulos and Richard Lukosius featured abstract art. More abstract art poured in, provoking a conflict with the traditionalists. Soon, any style and medium, including representational, would adorn the walls.

More programs and organizations utilized the Art Center: flower shows, antique shows, candlelight balls, poetry readings, theater, craft shows and Halloween parties. The Mystic Arts Café has scheduled literary readings and music since 1994. Visit them at: www.artscafemystic.org

In 1978, the Artists Balls were revived. In 1979, the first photography exhibit took place. In 1980, young artists displayed their work. By 1981, the Art Center opened five months of the year. Fund raising to repair the Center, now half a century old, became imperative. Grants, shows, Artists Balls, art auctions and concerts all contributed to maintain the building and rebuild the retaining wall along the Mystic River. By 1984, membership in the Association had reached 800. By 1986, six shows spread the season to six months. By the 1990's, the Mystic Art Center began to be open year round. It is part of the Mystic River Historic District. Please visit them at: wwwmysticarts.org or call: 860-536-7601.

MYSTIC & NOANK LIBRARY 1893

MYSTIC AND NOANK LIBRARY

40 Library Street, Mystic, Connecticut 06355

Elihu Spicer was born in Noank in1825. He went to sea as a boy and, by age twenty-two, had become captain of the bark *Fanny*. Thereafter, he skippered numerous vessels in round the world trade. I 1861 he joined with Charles H. Mallory of Mystic to form C. H. Mallory and Company. Elihu Spicer prospered.

He determined to build a library for Mystic across from his summer home on Elm Street. William Bigelow of New York designed the building; William Higginson supervised the construction. Work began the summer of 1892. The edifice was dedicated 23 January 1894. Elihu Spicer didn't live to see the dedication. He died 15 February 1893.

The library was constructed of Roman brick of a yellow ochre hue, highlighted by sienna red sandstone from Longmeadow, MA. The granite for the foundation came from Leete's Island, CT. The marble for the staircase and window casements and friezes came from VT, from TN, from Numidia. The roof was made of Roman tile. Italian tile mosaics were used in some floors. The interior wood paneling, coffers, doors and trim were of polished oak.

The initial collection of books numbered 4000. They were housed on the second floor. The first floor was reserved for a meeting room, in which 400 people gathered for the dedication. Over the years, both floors of the library gradually filled with books. By the 1980's, the Board of Trustees decided to expand. A fund raising campaign resulted in a 6000 square foot addition plus restoration of the original building. Architect Charles King of Avon, CT, successfully combined the old and new portions. The library dedicated the addition in December 1991. The ground floor of the addition houses the children's library plus a meeting room. The second floor houses non-fiction plus offices.

The library is part of the Mystic River Historic District.

The Friends of the Library organized in 1979. They organize book fairs and book discussion groups and literary readings. Their fund raising events have provided the library with computers, a microfilm machine, and projection equipment. Their newsletter, *Bookends*, a bimonthly, is mailed to its many members. Please visit the library at: www.mysticnoanklibrary.com or call: 860-536-7721.

UNION BAPTIST CHURCH

119 High Street, Mystic, Connecticut 06355

After the War of 1812, shipbuilding and commerce increased in Mystic. In 1819, the first bridge crossed the Mystic River. The new bridge and commercial prosperity brought more people to Mystic, but local churches were long walks away. In those days, there were the First Congregational Road Church in Stonington – built 1829 and still in use; the First Baptist Church in Mystic [Old Mystic] – built 1718 - used until 1843; and the Second Baptist Church on Fort Hill Road in Groton - built 1785 - used until 1843 - razed in 1908.

In 1828, subscriptions were taken to build a new church in Mystic – the Mariners' Free Church. It was stipulated that the church be open and free to any Christian. Only subscribers could vote on church business, but any were free to attend. A more common practice in those days was to rent or sell pews to raise funds. Of 172 subscribers, or proprietors, of the Mariners' Free Church, 80 commanded vessels. Deacon Erastus Gallup of Ledyard designed this imposing church.

Baptists, Methodists, and Congregationalists shared this new building in Portersville. Ministers of each sect took turns to deliver the service. In 1841, the Methodists built a church across the river in Mystic Bridge. In 1843, the First Baptists relocated to the center of Old Mystic and built a new church, and the Second Baptists closed their church on Fort Hill and built one near the Mariners' Free Church on High Street. In 1847, the Congregationalists built a new church across the river.

The Third Baptists, now in control of the Mariners' Free Church, merged with the Second Baptists. In 1861, the Second Baptist meetinghouse was dragged by oxen to the site and spliced to the back of the Mariners' Free Church at right angles. This present configuration became known as the Union Baptist Church.

During the Hurricane of 1938, the steeple of the Union Baptist Church was destroyed. Eventually funds were raised to replace it in 1969. At this time, a carillon was installed. Its lovely chimes can be heard throughout the village spread below. Union Baptist Church is part of the Mystic River Historic District

For more information about this American Baptist Church and its congregation, please visit www.ubcmystic.org or call: 860-536-9659

MYSTIC RIVER BRIDGE

Stonington to Groton via U. S. Route 1, Mystic, CT

Mystic, Connecticut, is another of those anomalies: a village split between two townships. The west bank, the Groton side, once was known as Portersville; in 1851, they began to call it Mystic River. The east bank of the Mystic River, the Stonington side, was known as Lower Mystic. After they bridged the river, it came to be known as Mystic Bridge. Now both halves of the village are known as Mystic.

In 1664, Robert Burrows began the first ferry above the present site of Mystic Seaport. Joseph Packer operated a later service, begun in 1769, at the end of the New London Road, behind what is now the Emporium [page 120] on Water Street.
.

By 1819, the first wooden bridge crossed the river bearing the Boston Post Road – today's U. S. Route 1. This privately owned bridge charged a toll: $.02 for pedestrians; $.25 for a coach. In 1841, Amos Clift rebuilt the bridge with a lift span raised by oxen. In 1854, Groton and Stonington purchased the bridge and removed the toll. These early bridges were built of wood and could not stand up to increasing traffic, heavy loads, and vibration. "Trot not on the bridge," read a current sign, later revised to "Walk your horses." In 1866, A. A. Briggs from Massachusetts built an iron swing bridge. In 1904, a sturdier swing bridge of steel was installed, but continual trolley traffic caused its foundations to settle. In 1922, new foundations were built and the present-day, efficient bascule bridge was erected.

Designed and patented by NY engineer, Thomas E. Brown, the bridge and counterweights are so well balanced that only two 36 horsepower motors can raise the bascule span in half a minute. An automated braking system arrests the span when it reaches the open position.

Built by the American Bridge Company of Philadelphia, the new bridge opened to the public 19 July 1922 with significant pomp and fanfare. The quarter million dollars were well spent. Nearly ninety years later, the Brown Balance Beam Light Bridge opens twelve times per day, six months of the year for river traffic.

The National Register of Historic Places designated the bridge and village an historic district in 1979.

MYSTIC SEAPORT

MYSTIC SEAPORT LIGHTHOUSE

75 Greenmanville Avenue, Mystic, Connecticut 06355

41° 21.69' North, 71° 58.02' West

This former site of the George Greenman & Co. boatyard, founded 1837, lies on the east bank of the Mystic River. Jutting into the river is a point of land on which perches a working replica of the Brant Point Lighthouse of Nantucket. The Seaport Light, built in 1966, also bears a similar fourth-order Fresnel lens. The Seaport Light, though merely 25' tall, is functional and active, though not official. It is open to the public, as are the numerous exhibits and the 19th century village. The blacksmith shop, cooper's shop, chandlery, shipping office, and bank are among the 30 or more authentic shops imported to the Seaport.

Among the vessels displayed at the Seaport are four that are National Historic Landmarks: whaler *Charles W. Morgan* [page 132], fishing schooner *L. A. Dunton,* Noank smack *Emma C. Berry*, and steamboat *Sabino*. Also worth visiting are the full-rigged training ship *Joseph Conrad* [page 134], replica schooner *Amistad*, and the beautiful schooner *Brilliant*. The Seaport is part of the Mystic Historic District.

The Henry B. duPont Preservation Shipyard is the focus of the Seaport. This facility has built and restored wooden vessels since the 1970's. The schooner *Amistad* was built here and launched in 2000, and whaler *Charles W. Morgan* is currently undergoing restoration, with a view to making her seaworthy.

Mystic Seaport came about through the efforts of three men. In 1929, Carl C. Cutler, Charles K. Stillman, and Edward Bradley incorporated the Marine Historical Association. Since then, Mystic Seaport, "the museum of America and the sea," has grown to become the most renowned maritime museum in the nation. Her collection of vessels [nearly 500], photographs [over 1,000,000] and maritime artifacts [about 2,000,000] is unsurpassed. The Treworgy Planetarium, the art gallery, gift shop, and maritime bookstore should not be missed. Neither should the permanent exhibits, which include figureheads, lighthouses, navigation, and ship models.

For information visit www.mysticseaport.org or call 888-973-2767 or 860-572-5315 for general information, or 860-572-0711 for visitor services.

CHARLES W. MORGAN

This wooden whaler was built in New Bedford, Massachusetts by Jethro and Zachariah Hillman and launched 21 July, 1841. The Quaker whaling merchant, Charles W. Morgan, paid over forty-eight thousand dollars for her. Today she resides at Mystic Seaport, last of a fleet of whaling ships that, in its heyday, in 1846, had 736 vessels. Her design of full rigged ship – having square sails on all three masts – was modified in 1867 to bark rig – having a gaff rigged fore and aft sail on the mizzenmast.

In her maiden voyage, which lasted over three years, the Morgan paid for herself. Over the 80 years during which she was worked, she made thirty-seven voyages in the Pacific, south Atlantic, and Indian oceans. She was the most remunerative whaling ship ever built in the U. S. A.

Her cargo consisted of oil for lighting and lubrication; spermaceti for candles; baleen, or whalebone, for corset stays or any application needing flexible material. By the end of the 19th century, petroleum mostly replaced oil from whales. Steam driven ships and harpoons shot from cannon hunted whales nearly to extinction. Whaling was officially prohibited in this country on 31 December 1971.

But the Morgan's work was done by the 1920's. She was preserved by Whaling Enshrined, Incorporated, and exhibited at the Green Estate in South Dartmouth, Massachusetts until November of 1941. In that year she was brought to Mystic Seaport. Here she was hauled, refitted, repaired, and re-rigged. Over the past 69 years, much of the Morgan above the waterline has been replaced. At present, she is on dry land at the Seaport undergoing extensive rebuilding.

Over the past three generations, she has been a showpiece of Mystic Seaport. Open to the public, she shares with them her part of history. Though the killing of whales is much to be deplored, it constituted a huge economic venture in southern New England, and provided oil for lighting millions of homes. The industry employed thousands of men, both whalers and ship builders; sail makers and coopers; blacksmiths and sawyers. The Secretary of the Interior declared her a National Historic Landmark on 21 July 1967.

For information visit www.mysticseaport.org or call 888-973-2767 or 860-572-5315 for general information, or 860-572-0711 for visitor services.

JOSEPH CONRAD

This square rigged, three masted, iron ship was built in Copenhagen in 1882 by Burmeister and Wain and lauched as *Georg Stage*, after the deceased son of ship owner Frederik Stage. The 111-foot ship was designed to train eighty boys at a time for the Danish merchant service. Until her sale in 1934, over 4000 cadets trained aboard her in the Baltic and North Seas. In 1905, a British freighter ran her down and sank her, drowning 22 boys. *Georg Stage* was raised and continued service.

Australian author and sailor Alan Villiers saved her from the scrap yard in 1934. He renamed her *Joseph Conrad* and, manning her mostly with boys, sailed her from Ipswich, England west around the world and to New York – a total distance of 57,000 miles. He arrived in New York, bankrupt, in 1936, and sold the ship to George Huntington Hartford, founder of the Great Atlantic & Pacific Tea Company [the A & P].

Hartford added an engine and used her as a private yacht until 1939, when he transferred her to the Maritime Commission to be used as a training vessel. In 1945, she was retired from this service and laid up for repairs. In 1947, through an act of Congress, she became part of the Mystic Seaport collection, where she presently resides.

Joseph Conrad, for whom she is named, was a Pole born in the Russian Ukraine in 1857. He served in both the French and English merchant marines, earning both his Master Mariners certificate and his British citizenship in 1886. As a British citizen, he perfected his mastery of the English language and began to write. He produced such classics as *Lord Jim, The Secret Agent*, and *Nostromo*. These were more than just romantic fiction. They were psychological studies that plumbed the fathomless depths of the human soul. As captain of a Congo steamboat in 1889, he witnessed atrocities in the Congo Free State that inspired his great work, *Heart of Darkness*. After sixteen years in the merchant navy, he retired from the sea in 1894 to pursue his writing. By the time of his death in 1924, Conrad had earned the recognition of the literary world.

Joseph Conrad now resides at a pier at Mystic Seaport. Her duties entail being an exhibit for Seaport visitors, and being a static training ship for the Mystic Mariner Program. I made this illustration from a photo I took one spring from my kayak on the Mystic River when the *Conrad's* masts had been pulled. Visit *Joseph Conrad* at www.mysticseaport.org

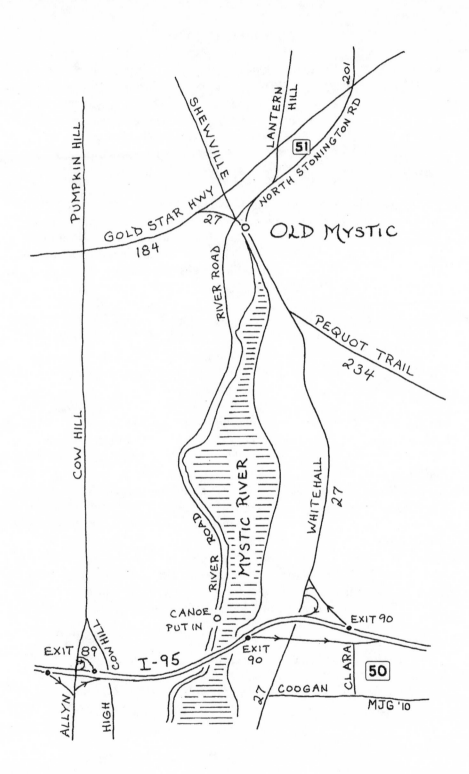

OLD MYSTIC

#50	**MYSTIC AQUARIUM**
#51	**CLYDE'S CIDER MILL**

MYSTIC AQUARIUM & INSTITUTE for EXPLORATION

55 Coogan Boulevard, Mystic, Connecticut 06355

Industrial and philanthropist Kelvin Smith was Mystic Aquarium Corporation's major shareholder when it opened in 1973 as a private business. In 1999, the Ballard Institute for Exploration merged with the Aquarium. Their combined efforts utilized $52,000,000 to build an Arctic coast exhibit, featuring an acre of outdoor salt pond to house Beluga whales. Steller sea lions, California sea lions, and Northern fur seals are provided outdoor pools. The underwater portions of all these pools can be viewed from within the building through huge plate glass windows. Other pools and enclosures feature several species of penguins. Feeding the whales always draws an audience outdoors. The whale trainer puts these gentle creatures through their paces, then flings them mullet by the fistful.

Within the building, the first, large cylindrical tank contains jellyfish. The original shape shifters, jellyfish are beautiful, and rhythmic; colorful and subtle. The sharks, nearby, circle their barely adequate tank as would a greyhound locked in a small apartment. The Manta and stingrays are nearly as graceful as seals. The cow rays, in their petting tank, come by to have their ears scratched. The cod and hake and haddock in the North Atlantic tank give a fresh perspective to the lifeless fillets we see when buying dinner. The octopus can seldom be seen; he squeezes his bulk between the rocks in his tank. The numerous smaller aquariums hold mostly exotic species. The sea lions at the amphitheater will leave you smiling. In exchange for mullet, they roll over and clap and juggle and dive and jump through hoops. Their ultimate stunt is to dive deep into the pool, then launch themselves vertically in a water-clearing leap.

Dr. Robert Ballard, founder of the Institute for Exploration, specializes in deep-sea archeology and discovered the RMS Titanic. A room is dedicated to this proud ship, and a huge model of the vessel is on display. Another well-documented wreck at the Institute is that of Lt. John Kennedy's PT-109. Exonerated of responsibility for colliding with a Japanese ship, he displayed prudence and heroism.

The Aquarium is open year round and features hands on summer camps for families and children ages 2-16, and veterinary internships for college students. Please visit: www.mysticaquarium.org or call 860-572-5955.

B.F.
CLYDE'S CIDER MILL ESTAB.
1881

MJG '70

B. F. CLYDE'S CIDER MILL - 1881

129 North Stonington Road, Stonington, CT 06355

Oldest steam powered cider mill in the USA

Family owned for 6 generations

When you step inside this small building while milling is underway, the heady aroma of apples will delight you. Old fashioned, overhead belting slaps at the pulleys; the mill rotates; cider streams from the press. Everything is sparkling clean and the pulleys are brightly painted. A knowledgeable person will conduct you and explain the process.

Afterwards, you can go to the quaint store close by and purchase apples, several varieties of apple wine, apple butter, fresh apple donuts, apple pies, and pumpkin bread; pumpkins, gourds, local honey and maple syrup, and a variety of jams, jellies and condiments. Both hot and cold cider is served, and the various apple wines can be sampled. There are also Clyde's ball caps and tee shirts.

A small gristmill stands on the premises, and freshly milled Johnnycake flour is available, as well as Indian corn and kettle corn.

There are tables and chairs on the porch where you can relax and enjoy your cider and donuts. Weekends in pleasant weather there is often a small band on the lawn playing country music beneath the shade of the venerable maples.

Milling demonstrations are held Saturdays and Sundays during October and November. The store is open seven days a week from September to late December.

Clyde's is one of only eight sites in Connecticut designated an Historic Mechanical Engineering Landmark.

Check Clyde's website, www.bfclydescidermill.com for further information, directions, and videos on cider making, or call: 860-536-3354.

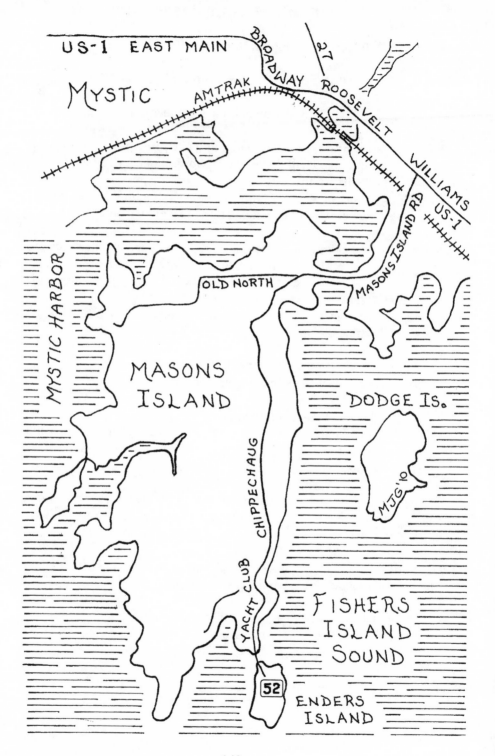

MASONS ISLAND

#52

CHAPEL OF OUR LADY OF THE ASSUMPTION

CHAPEL OF OUR LADY OF THE ASSUMPTION

Saint Edmund's Retreat

Yacht Club Road, Ender's Island, Mystic, Connecticut 06355

Thomas B. Enders was born in Hartford and took a medical degree in 1892 from The College of Physicians and Surgeons in New York. After he retired from practice, he bought an eleven-acre island by the sea from the Sisters of Charity and commenced to build an estate. After his death, his wife, Alys VanGuilder Enders, determined to leave her property to the church. In 1954, the Society of Saint Edmund began a noviate there.

Saint Edmond was born Edmond Rich in 1175 at Abingdon, England, a few miles from Oxford. He studied at Oxford and Paris and became professor of mathematics and dialectics at both universities about 1200. Due in part to his pious upbringing, he determined to become a priest, became ordained, took a doctorate in divinity, and became professor of theology at Oxford. Tiring of scholasticism, he left Oxford and, for eleven years, acted as treasurer of Salisbury Cathedral. He began to preach, inciting people to embark on the 6th Crusade in 1227. In 1233, Pope Gregory IX appointed him Archbishop of Canterbury. His conflicts with King Henry III, son of King John, and his differences with the Pope concerning the autonomy of the English Church led him to retire to the Abbey of Pontigny in France about 1240. He died shortly after at the Priory of Soisy. His life of asceticism, self-sacrifice and devotion led to his canonization in 1247.

The Reverend Jean Baptiste Muard founded the Society of Saint Edmund at Pontigny in 1843. They are an order of priests and brothers who foster spiritual renewal, evangelization, and social justice. The name Edmund in Old English means "happy protection."

By the 1970's, the need for novitiates had so decreased that Enders Island began to provide retreats for laity and clergy alike; retreats for families, for recovery, or for spiritual distress. St. Edmunds also host classes on the art of illumination; concerts; and literary readings.

Visitors are always welcome. The view of the sea is inspiring. The Chapel of Our Lady of the Annunciation is a peaceful place to reflect. Please visit: www.endersisland.com or call: 860-536-7601.

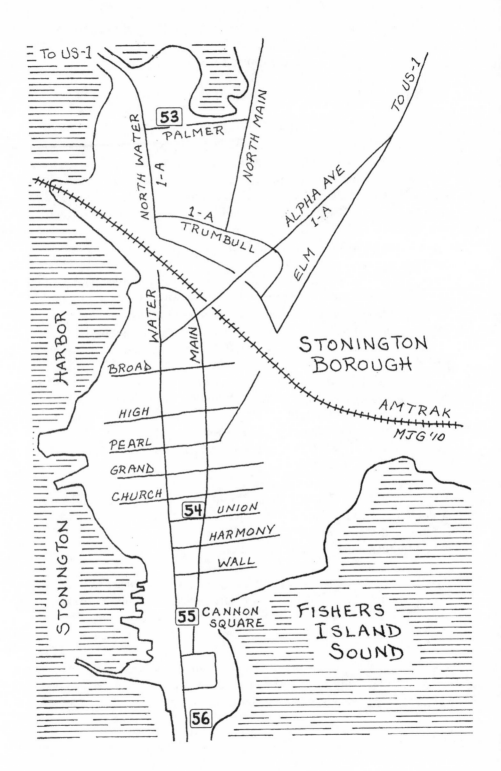

TO US-1

53 PALMER

NORTH WATER

1-A

NORTH MAIN

TO US-1

ALPHA AVE

1-A TRUMBULL

1-A

ELM

HARBOR

WATER

MAIN

BROAD

HIGH

PEARL

GRAND

CHURCH

54 UNION

HARMONY

WALL

55 CANNON SQUARE

56

STONINGTON

STONINGTON BOROUGH

AMTRAK
MJG '10

FISHERS ISLAND SOUND

STONINGTON BOROUGH

#53	**CAPTAIN PALMER HOUSE**
#54	**FIRST BAPTIST CHURCH**
#55	**CANNON SQUARE**
#56	**STONINGTON LIGHTHOUSE MUSEUM**

CAPTAIN NATHANIEL B. PALMER HOUSE

40 Palmer Street, Stonington, CT 06378

Nathaniel Brown Palmer [1799-1877] was born in Stonington. He and his brother, Alexander Smith Palmer, [1806-1894] became sea captains at early ages. Nat Palmer, the twenty-one-year-old skipper of the 47' sloop, *Hero*, was part of a sealing fleet that sailed so far to the south that he spotted land not found on his chart. It was understood, later, that he had sighted Antarctica. Larger ships skippered by von Bellingshausen and Bransfield reported seeing portions of this land earlier in 1820. Though Palmer did not sight land until 17 November 1820, he supposedly was the first to go ashore. A portion of the mainland is known today as Palmer Land, and there is also a Palmer Archipelago, and a Palmer Station. A clipper ship, the N. B. Palmer, was named for him as well as an icebreaker, RV Nathaniel B. Palmer.

During the next two decades the Palmer brothers skippered fast clipper ships to the Orient, sometimes setting records for rapid passage. Captain Nat designed some of his ships. Captain Alexander was famed for his rescue of the crews of two imperiled ships; Queen Victoria awarded him a gold medal. During the 1840's and 50's, Captain Nat owned shares in some of the fastest clippers in the trade.

On retiring, they built a modern, Victorian home of sixteen rooms, *Pine Point*, in Stonington in 1853. The fashionable New York architect, Gamaliel King, designed it. The transitional style, between *Greek Revival* and *Victorian Italianate*, is simple and attractive. On a rise, it overlooks the upper reach of Stonington harbor. Within, the craftsmanship reminds you that the carpenters were boatwrights. The intricate ceiling moldings and spiral staircase by which to ascend to the cupola are exquisite. The rooms are bright and sunny.

Threatened with demolition, the Palmer house found new life as headquarters of the Stonington Historical Society, which purchased it in 1994. The National Register of Historic Places listed the Palmer House in 1996, and also designated it a National Historic Landmark.

The Palmer House and Lighthouse Museum [page 154] in Stonington Borough are under the aegis of the Stonington Historical Society and open to the public May till October. One ticket gains admittance to both. For more information, visit www.stoningtonhistory.org or call the Society at 860-535-8445.

FIRST BAPTIST CHURCH – 1889

50 Main Street, Stonington, Connecticut 06378

The First Baptist society in Stonington Borough was organized in 1772. By 1794 they had built a church on Water Street. In 1835, they replaced it. On 1 July 1889, the Reverend D. Henry Miller officiated at laying the cornerstone of a new church at the corner of Main and Union Street. The older church on Water Street was razed.

The new church would remain in service until 1950. At this time, the diminished congregation merged with that of the 2nd Congregational Church at the corner of Main and Elm Street to form the United Church of Stonington.

In 1957, the Baptist Church building was sold to Charles Fuller, an architect, and his wife Anne. They removed the projecting portion of the nave and added a veranda. They used the foundation stones to enclose their garden and to build a patio. In addition to making it their home, Anne Fuller converted part of the church to an art gallery. The pyramid shaped steeple on the bell tower had already been destroyed by a hurricane.

In 1968, the church was sold to Inger McCabe Elliot, a photojournalist, to be her private residence.

Originally, the shingled siding was coated with linseed oil and turpentine and allowed to attain a weathered patina. At present, the church is painted white with blue trim. It is readily viewed from Main and Union Streets.

CANNON SQUARE
STONINGTON
CONNECTICUT

CANNON SQUARE

1 Cannon Square, Stonington, Connecticut 06378

On 9 August 1814, Commodore Sir Thomas Hardy approached Stonington Harbor with a squadron of English warships: *Ramillies*, 74 guns; frigate *Pactolus*, 44 guns; brigs *Dispatch & Nimrod*, 20 guns each; & bomb ship *Terror*. On demanding the surrender of the village, he received the reply: "We shall defend the place to the last extremity; should it be destroyed, we shall perish in its ruins." Provoked by this rebuff, *Dispatch* and *Terror* bombarded the Borough for three days. One American fatality was recorded, a mortally ill old woman.

The Americans trained one cannon on *Dispatch* and exacted retaliation. With the second cannon, loaded with grapeshot, they repulsed a landing party. On 12 August, the English squadron departed with their casualties. The residents erected a small brownstone monument in front of the old library at Church Street and Main, listing the names of the prominent defenders of the Borough. In 1876, the villagers petitioned Congress for the two, 18 pound cannons instrumental in saving their town. They placed them on the tiny Town Square, which since has been known as Cannon Square. The monument was removed, placed between the guns, and topped by a cannon ball.

The British bombardment in 1814 plus two severe fires in the 1830's destroyed the original buildings surrounding the square. Today, on the north side stands #3 Cannon Square - the former Ocean Bank – a Greek Revival marble structure built in 1851 - now Bank of America, and, next door, at #2, the Tuscan Style home of the former bank manager, Gurdon Pendleton, built in 1848. On the east side, pictured here, runs Main Street. From left to right are: #11, the Capt. Billings Burtch House – 1876; #9, a stone house built in 1941; and #7, the Greek Revival Gurdon Trumbull House – 1840. To the south, at #1 Cannon Square, former site of the Borough Hotel, stands a Second Empire House. To the west, on Water Street, lies a parking lot.

Cannon Square is undergoing restoration. The canons, cast in Salisbury, Ct in 1781, have been sent to Texas A & M University for restoration. Black iron posts and a chain fence will surround the square, the land be reseeded, and a handicapped ramp improve accessibility.

For information visit www.stoningtonhistory.org or call 860-535-8445.

STONINGTON HARBOR LIGHT
STONINGTON
CONNECTICUT
1840

OLD LIGHTHOUSE MUSEUM

Stonington Point - 7 Water Street, Stonington, CT 06378

The original Stonington Light, built in 1823, was powered by ten whale oil lamps and parabolic reflectors, and was visible from twelve miles out to sea. It stood on Windmill Point, on the west side of Stonington Harbor. By 1840, erosion posed a serious threat to the structure, and the present lighthouse across the harbor on Stonington Point was built using materials from the elder. In 1856, a new 6th order Fresnel lens was installed. The focal plane was sixty-two feet above the sea, although the octagon granite tower stands only 32.5 feet high.

In 1889, a 25-foot, iron lighthouse was built on the new west breakwater, and the granite lighthouse was decommissioned. The building continued as the light keeper's residence until 1908 when a new one was constructed. In 1926, a skeleton light tower replaced the breakwater lighthouse, which was later demolished by the hurricane of 1938.

In 1927, the Stonington Lighthouse became a museum under the auspices of the Stonington Historical Society. Its six rooms display portraits and artifacts depicting Stonington's rich, 360-year history. Fishing, whaling, farming, trading and the arts are all represented. From the tower, one can see Fishers Island, NY, Watch Hill, RI, and much of the nearby Connecticut shoreline.

In 1975, the National Register of Historic Places added Stonington Lighthouse.

The museum is presently open from May till October. Please call 860-535-1440 for hours and directions.

Stonington Historical Society also manages the Woolworth Library and the Captain Nathaniel B. Palmer House at 40 Palmer Street [page 148]. Admission to both the Lighthouse Museum and the Nathaniel Palmer House can be secured with a single pass. The Society's brochure, "An Hour's Walk through the Borough of Stonington, Connecticut," is well worth owning. Contact them at 860-535-8445 or visit them at: www.stoningtonhistory.org